Greenhill
Books

# DIARY OF A
# DEAD OFFICER

ARTHUR GRAEME WEST

# DIARY OF A
# DEAD OFFICER

Being the Posthumous Papers
of Arthur Graeme West

Introduced by Nigel Jones

Greenhill Books, London
MBI Publishing, St Paul

Greenhill
Books

*Diary of a Dead Officer*
*Being the Posthumous Papers of Arthur Graeme West*

This edition published in 2007 by Greenhill Books/Lionel Leventhal Ltd
Park House, 1 Russell Gardens, London NW11 9NN
and
MBI Publishing Co.
Galtier Plaza, Suite 200, 380 Jackson Street, St Paul, MN 55101-3885, USA

*British Library Cataloguing-in Publication Data*
West, Arthur Graeme
Diary of a dead officer : being the posthumous papers of
Arthur Graeme West
1. West, Arthur Graeme – Diaries
2. World War, 1914–1918 – Campaigns – France
3. World War, 1914–1918 – Personal narratives, British
I. Title

940.4'8141'092

ISBN 978-1-85367-729-8

*Library of Congress Cataloging-in Publication Data available*

*Publishing History*
*Diary of a Dead Officer* was first published in 1919 by Allen & Unwin,
and included an introduction by Cyril Joad.

For more information on our books, please visit www.greenhillbooks.com,
email sales@greenhillbooks.com, or telephone us within the UK on 020 8458
6314. You can also write to us at the above London address.

Designed and typeset by MATS Typesetters, Essex

Printed and bound in Great Britain by
Creative Print and Design (Wales), Ebbw Vale

# CONTENTS

# Introduction

Anyone who knows anything about the First World War knows the story of Siegfried Sassoon and his protest against the conduct of the conflict. Indeed, so familiar has the tale become that it is now the stuff of literary legend: embroidered by the soldier poet himself, by his then friend, regimental comrade and fellow poet Robert Graves; and subsequently on stage by Stephen Macdonald in his play 'Not About Heroes' and in fiction and film in Pat Barker's novel trilogy 'Regeneration', which takes the story on to Sassoon's meeting with his fellow poet and protégé, Wilfred Owen. Sassoon and Owen, of course, *are* the First World War for many people today. Thanks to their ubiquitous presence on the school curriculum, the pacifist poets of protest and pity are familiar, perhaps overfamiliar, figures. Very few, however, it can be confidently stated, have heard of Arthur

Graeme West, the author of the present book. And yet there are clear and interesting parallels with Sassoon's better known but far less tragic story. West, like Sassoon, was a withdrawn public school and Oxbridge boy whose shy diffidence concealed firm, even fierce opinions. West, like Sassoon, was an enthusiastic, early volunteer for the war, underwent a long period of home training, but was speedily disillusioned both with the Army and with the wider war. West, like Sassoon, came under the influence of pacifists while on home leave, particularly that iconic intellectual poster-boy of the pacifist cause, Bertrand Russell. (In Sassoon's case, directly, when they met at the pacifists' unofficial HQ and salon, Garsington Manor, the home of Russell's lover Lady Ottoline Morrell; in West's case more indirectly – he avidly read Russell's anti-war tracts 'Justice in War Time' and 'Principles of Social Reconstruction' [1916], and subsequently corresponded with the philosopher.) Finally, West, like Sassoon, made up his mind during a period of home leave to refuse further service in the war. But here we come to the crucial difference between the two men: while Sassoon went ahead with his protest, amidst the full glare of a publicity campaign orchestrated by his influential pacifist friends; West, as this diary so agonisingly and poignantly relates, 'bottled out' at the last moment; retrieved the letter to his Commanding Officer informing him of his decision to refuse any further part in the war, and, with a sort of sullen, fatal resignation, returned to the trenches, and to his death. West's failure of nerve is all the more striking since his rejection of the war and all its works was far more ferocious and radical than Sassoon's mild and gentlemanly cry of complaint. West's *cri de coeur*, by contrast, reaches a height of pure, almost childlike, screeching rage. On August 16th, in the summer of the bloody battle of the Somme, West, on leave and visiting his militantly pacifist friend C.E.M. Joad, on Box Hill in Surrey, wrote: 'If the war were to begin tomorrow and were to find me as I am now, I would not join the Army, and if I had the courage I would desert now . . . What right has anybody to demand of me that I should give up my chance of obtaining happiness – the only chance I have, and the only thing worth obtaining here? Because they are foolish enough – not reasonable enough – to give their own up, that is no reason why I should abandon mine. I asked no one to form societies to help me exist. I certainly asked no one to start this war.'

The person from whom this shriek of extreme individualism was wrung had always been a loner; a withdrawn personality who even his friends found difficult to fully fathom. Born in Norfolk on September 23rd, 1891, West was the eldest of four children of another Arthur West, a retired missionary, of typically narrow and unbending Victorian religiosity. Their mother died young, and West was brought up in Highgate in what seems to have been a joyless atmosphere, shielding his younger siblings from their stern father, at least until 1905 when Arthur Snr. remarried, the family relocated to a large house in Regent's Park, and West was promptly packed off to Blundell's, an ancient West Country boarding school. Here he met and fell under the influence of his lifelong friend, Cyril Joad, the intellectual star of the school. After Joad, to no one's surprise, won the school's scholarship to Balliol College, Oxford, in 1909, West – to general astonishment – won it the following year. At Oxford he pursued his quietly individualistic course, studying the Classics, reading the great works of English literature and preparing, like hundreds of others at the university, for an unremarkable career in teaching, the Civil Service or some similar humdrum profession (doubtless to his father's distress, he seems to have lost his Christian faith). In August 1914, all those futures became impossible. Joad, beginning a lifelong career as an opinionated contrarian, instantly plunged in to swim against the prevailing patriotic tide by proclaiming the war 'criminal folly'. West, always his own man, tried, equally instantly, to join up. Joad's brief biographical introduction to the first edition of *Diary of a Dead Officer* (1918/19) misleadingly gives the impression that West was his pacifist clone and immediately repented of his moment of madness in joining up. This was, it is now clear, far from the case. Nowhere does Joad mention that West had been a member of the Oxford Officers' Training Corps throughout his four years at the University; nor does he suggest the repeated efforts that West made to get into the ranks after his initial application had been rejected because of poor eyesight. Although West seems a far from natural soldier, with his scholarly untidiness, his aversion to sport and his stubborn individualism,

11

he finally succeeded in joining the Public Schools
Battalion in February 1915 and became a lance
corporal. By 1916 he was at the front in France.
1916, the year of the Somme, was the watershed
year for West, as it was for the British Army as a
whole. His front line experience was distilled in
his two finest poems: 'The Night Patrol' written
in March – a description of a nocturnal voyage
into a no-man's-land where the only guiding
markers are corpses in various stages of
decomposition – and 'God! How I hate you, you
young cheerful men' in which he excoriated the
patriotic poems of an Oxford contemporary Rex
Freston who had been killed in action. Both
works are remarkable for their accuracy of
observation; their candid, almost exultant, des-
criptions of the horrors of the trenches, and the
angry extremity of their disillusion: he is as
scornful of the 'pious poetry' produced by dead
patriotic poets, despite their having 'been to
France,/And seen the trenches, glimpsed the
huddled dead/In the periscope, hung in the
rusting wire:/Choked by their sickly foetor, day
and night/Blown down his throat . . . Perhaps/
Had seen a man killed, a sentry shot at night,/
Hunched as he fell, his feet on the firing-

step,/His neck against the back slope of the trench,/And the rest doubled up between, his head/Smashed like an egg-shell, and the warm grey brain/Spattered all bloody on the parados'. Lines like this made even Sassoon's bitter squibs of disillusionment read tamely. And, like Sassoon, West dares to mock the pieties of religion, as well as those of patriotism: 'Ah, how good God is/To suffer us be born just now, when youth/That else would rust, can slake his blade in gore,/Where very God Himself does seem to walk/The bloody fields of Flanders He so loves!' In April 1916 West was accepted for an officer-training course. His description of his time at a grim training camp in Scotland deserves a place in any anthology of army life – rarely can the bleak, pointless culture of bull, bullying and the sheer mind-numbing tedium of the non-combatant military life have been more ruthlessly skewered. West's resentment of the 'dug-outs' – superannuated drillmasters brought out of retirement to bawl out the officer cadets – is especially marked. It is at this point that his growing resentments, against the Army, the War, the Establishment and God Himself – in the increasingly unlikely event of His existence – seem to curdle

13

and coalesce into a fierce rage against West's place in the universe. But, despite it all, he passes his course, and is commissioned as a subaltern in the 'Ox and Bucks', the Oxfordshire and Buckinghamshire Light Infantry. It is now, before returning to France as an officer, that West experiences the supreme crisis of his young life. Influenced by his eager readings of Russell's pacifist books, by his love affair with a radical young woman, by his tender relationship with his sister and, also, by the radical urgings of Joad and his bride whose Box Hill home became a home from home for West, as Garsington had been for Sassoon, West wrote a letter to his C.O. renouncing the war and any further part in it. According to one account he even posted it, but recalled it from the postman before it was collected. At any rate, he reluctantly returned to his base in Wareham, Dorset, still reading Russell on the train and cursing the war. On April 3rd, 1917, West was on duty in a front line trench near Bapaume for early morning 'Stand To!'; that fraught period when the rising sun in the east blinded the British to what their enemy was up to, and men stood ready with loaded guns and fixed bayonets, poised to repel any surprise enemy assault. That morning, the crack of a sniper's rifle split the silence and Arthur Graeme West, as he had surely foreseen, died. He was buried near where he fell.

West's friend Joad, by then a militant pacifist, conceived it as his duty to memorialise his friend as cut from the same cloth. His edited edition of West's army diaries, and the handful of poems he left, was published within weeks of the war's ending in an edition sponsored by the Socialist Daily Herald newspaper (West's younger brother later became a Communist). Although it is clear – as any reading of *Diary of a Dead Officer* will instantly show – that West rejected the war, this was less from idealistic Joadian pacifist Christian principles, and much more from a very understandable desire to save his own life and go on living in a world, that, for all its random meaninglessness, he still enjoyed inhabiting. Young, in love, West's motivations were much the same as those of the millions of men who fought and died with him. More sensitive than most, he clearly felt the sounds, sights and smells of the trenches more deeply than thicker-skinned comrades. But to view him through Joad's eyes as a pacifist martyr would be to misunderstand him. West died as he lived – as his own man. All we have left is this savagely honest account of his wartime service. It is enough. Brief though it is, it sears itself into the memory, and marks West out as a writer of real quality, originality and independence of thought. To take just one passage – his account of unearthing comrades buried alive by a shell, and his finding them, the living, the dead and the mad, covered in soil like so many potatoes – is to realise what an outstanding witness of war we lost with West's death.

NIGEL JONES

# Part One – Diary

*West enlisted as a private early in 1915. The following extracts describe the impression produced upon him by his early acquaintance with Army life. It is to be regretted that the diary which he kept about this time is very scanty, and there is no record available of the general frame of mind in which he enlisted, and of his early and more pleasant experiences of the Army. In explanation of this there is an entry towards the close of 1915 in which he says:*

*"The earlier events of 1915 have to be put down here from memory in the briefest way, because I bought no diary, money being rare at the time. Lacking the stimulus to energy given by an allotted space to be filled daily, I never wrote. A perpetual undercurrent of search for a commission was the main thing, though on the surface life seemed much as usual."*

*There is no doubt, however, that West was very keen to join. His enthusiasm is shown by the persistence with which he pursued the commission which was refused him owing to defective eyesight, and the evident satisfaction with which he records getting passed by a private doctor, "more or less by ruse", when the regular recruiting doctor had ploughed him. For a time he was happy enough, finding congenial companions and buoyed up by the consciousness of having done the right thing, and it is a little unfortunate that the first important extract, dated March 22nd, contains some rather snobbish strictures on his companions, and conveys a general impression of discontent which was not typical of his attitude at the time.*

*In November of the same year he crossed to France.*

## ON JOINING THE ARMY AS A PRIVATE
## JAN. 1915

*Monday*, March 22nd, 1915.

The first and chief way in which these experiences offended me was by their irredeemable ugliness. This was horribly intensified, after some month and a half, towards the end of which I was often happy, by five of the "fæx Romuli" coming into the Hut and crowding the number up to over thirty. On Sunday, too (the day before this Monday), began an indefinite period of isolation for measles, and we were thrown together more. Marches, in which these five were anywhere within one's range of vision or smell (not perhaps that they impinged so unpleasantly on that sense by the uncleanliness of their persons as by the rankness of their cigarettes), stirred in me such a spirit of fermenting malignity that I would cheerfully have killed them. I never hated Army life so much. Their thick necks, whose lines were so graceless, that seen from behind there was a continuous, unbroken sweep from base of neck to crown, their big flapping ears, the inveterate curl under the hats, their insolent leering

21

expression, or their vaguely wretched stupidity was stirringly noisome, after the faces I was growing accustomed to as my own surroundings. I used to walk along – or I did this day – beside H..... and C....., who had left their positions to come by me, while the air, soft as milk, and as sweet, came past tainted by their vile cigarettes, the landscape, that seemed almost to complain that such as we three were could not visit and praise it as it deserved, being further dishonoured by these ugly presences, the companions of our constraint. If any more of these creatures come in and no change of Huts can be made, they will rise, like. H. G. Wells' Morlocks in the "Time Machine," from their position of excluded ugliness and possess the house. The attitude of the former hut-dwellers is universally hostile at present; and some of those whose own social position was, perhaps, not before very well assured are foremost in the underhand campaign of indignant protest.

## THE LAST TIME IN ENGLAND
### THE CHARING CROSS ROAD

*Monday*, Nov. 7th, 1915.

As I began the journey through the raw November night, returning to camp from this, my last week-end leave, it pleased me to picture all those other Saturdays and Sundays, from early spring until the late autumn, that I had spent when my station had been at W....., C....., or S.....

It chanced that as I lifted the blind for a last sight of London, the towers of Westminster sprang in clear outline from the indistinguishable mass of mean buildings between them and the railway, and so moulded my yet vague memories definitely to the journey from Victoria to North London. I remembered in an orderly detached way, as if it were another's experience I was contemplating, the thrill of first contact with London as I emerged from Victoria Station into the open square, looking for a north-bound 'bus. True I never felt free, never dreamt for a moment that the old days were back again, myself and the city were too deeply stained with war, but I gained here a comforting security that

23

the possibilities of my old life were being preserved, held in trust against the day when I should be able to resume them.

The shops, the advertisements, the people hurrying about the streets were evidence of the vitality of the former way of things.

And it was thus that the women pleased me especially, by their brave show of other concerns than the war. How delightful it was to mark the spreading of a new fashion, and how kindly one felt to this one or that who, with the new full skirt swinging high above her ankles, gave assurance of a bold prodigality, an open loyalty to a code which many affected in these days to despise.

But when the noisy patriotism of Trafalgar Square was left behind in the cool indifference of Charing Cross Road, I had usually, I smiled as I thought of it, left the 'bus and progressed in the fashion of a grazing heifer up that strangely-attractive street, which had always seemed to me to contain symbolically in itself all the experiences of human life. The books alone from Homer, Virgil and the oriental classics to the slim volume of modern verse, a few slight poems in lame metre and uncertain of expression, gave the suggestion of a vast literary republic stretching from the beginnings of Time until to-day, while the variety of sublime or trivial, Christian or pagan, homely or exotic, products of fine reason or depraved sensibility, were reduced here to a level of silent impotence, a dependence only on their appeal to something in the soul of some unknown buyer for their release from the dingy shelves.

## THE FIRST TIME IN FRANCE

### *Friday*, Nov. 26th, 1915.

We were all off parade in the morning and went into a small shed in the orchard, full of sacks of potatoes, and with the windows browned by smoke. I read the *Saturday Westminster Gazette*, others read or wrote. It was very jolly. We talked of the various ways of facing these experiences, whether to "glorify present experience" in the words of C....., or to dream utopias of one's own as A..... did. A....., as C..... read an epitaph on a "governess" out of the *S.W.G.*, remarked he wished he were a governess, and we built up a picture of a home in West

Kensington, nice children, a nursery, toasting at the fire, a young good-looking master . . .

No parade in the afternoon. Read the "Odyssey" and enjoyed it for itself and for the really novel exercise of making out the meaning of the lines and the new interest it gave to war.


## A FINE DAY

### *Tuesday*, Nov. 30th, 1915.

A very fine clear sunny day. We threw mangolds about all the morning as if they were bombs, and in the afternoon went a short march towards St. V..... The sunlight lay on the wet cobbles of the road as we came back, outlining all the horses and carts with watery gold. The bare trees against the almost colourless sky were exquisitely beautiful, and filled me with an indefinable desire for something beyond that, I remember, Mark Rutherford speaks of. It was not connected explicitly with the war or the chance of death; I have always felt it looking at such scenes, and then, with the possibility of speedy death before me, I understood more clearly than ever before that I had got from this particular impression all that could be got, that it was perfect, and could not by longer living be at all improved or developed. One's wonder at all these things, the forms of trees and the stars as I see them now at evening, is simply an elemental fact, permanently renewed and always mixed with that painful yearning that I felt then: it is a mistake to look for any enlightenment or to expect a time when one will somehow "understand it." It is not intellectual.

## THE FIRST TIME IN THE TRENCHES

### *Wednesday*, Dec. 7th, 1915.

Trenches. A day like yesterday, but wetter. Paraded at 3.30 in haversacks and water-bottle, groundsheet and leather jerkin for the trenches. Marched along a pretty bad road till dark, past an English Cemetery full of little wooden crosses, until we came to a very ruined village.

It was raining hard by now and we were wet already. We struck off across the open over old trenches for almost a mile. We were meant to go by communication trenches, but they were so full of water that we had to go on top. The mud and water were worse than anything we had ever met, many went in up to their necks, and all of us were soaked up to and over the knees.

We passed the supports and reserve-trenches with fires in braziers and many dugouts draped with groundsheets. In the support trench men were sleeping here and there outside, sitting on the firing platform in groundsheets. The trenches were wet but boarded at the bottom, so one did not walk in more than three or four inches of water. Our platoon was to go to the front-line trenches, which were not trenches at all, but broken bits of trench, the tolerably whole parts of which we held in sections of five. We five were together in post No. G at the extreme left end of that line. It was a very bad place; about ten or fifteen yards of sand-bags were standing, but the tops had been knocked off and the things were low. There was no back to the trench at all, and the water was deep; we had nothing to keep it off us but a few sticks laid across. We had no shelter from the rear or side at all. The general idea was that we were the front line and had to hold it until the supports came up. As there was a wire entanglement between us and the supports they would take a long time to come up and we ourselves should be wiped out; then the supports would be caught in the communication trench like rats in a trap, and killed off, too. Then the reserves would come into play, repulse the enemy and shell them out. The Germans were rather less than 200 yards off, too far to throw bombs, but snipers were active. Though no rifle-bullets ever came near us, the Germans had machine-guns trained along the top of the parapet, and they troubled us a good deal.

At first we were quite amused and laughed at our position, but soon the damp and cold and the prospect of twenty-four hours' endurance of it, our isolation and exposure cooled us down, and we sat still and dripped and shivered. Flares went up continually, and occasional machine-gun bullets whizzed over us, and snipers shot.

At 12.30 we were relieved by some of the X..... regiment and sent to Post No. 5. We had got more or less dry while at the other post, and now got wet again, but the change was worth it. Across the whole bit of trench we now had a shelter of corrugated iron, which covered about six feet of space. Bombs and ammunition were stored in a kind of recess here, and it was therefore dry, though water lay underfoot in the trench. It had stopped raining. We now sat down on boxes of ammunition, and I took my boots and socks and putties off, though my legs from the knees down remained like marble all the time. G..... passed during the night asking for reports. There were none from us. We slept little and put no guard; waking from short dozes with one's head leant back on the sand-bags of the side of the trench one saw a few stars, or the rising and falling light of a flare, and heard if a rifle or machine-gun fired.

## THOUGHTS ABOUT DEATH

*Undated.*

Death one regarded in many different ways, partly according as one's beliefs or convictions concerning an after state were bright or gloomy, partly according as one's love of life was intense or weak.

I have no real firmly settled beliefs as to what will happen after death, though sometimes I think of a lease of more vigorous energy on lines higher than the highest I have known her; though not very different in kind. I remember feeling this just before we left England, and it was then, of course, that death seemed least grim. Another and more common form of death as a welcome thing was when we were in the trenches and it was very cold and wet and dull then I was glad to put my head up above the parapet, thinking that a bullet there was a possibility, and no unwelcome one either; such feelings prompted action that might seem to be, but wasn't, courageous. Any ideas about personal meetings after death I never had. By far the commonest mood, then, was that I have mentioned, where death was a relief, most welcome in itself and of no positive significance at all. A slightly different emotional state was the purely fantastic, on the whole rather a happy state, and not necessarily associated with unpleasant circumstances; I could live quite happily and vigorously in it. It was the usual reply one gave to the question: *Of what use has all my elaborate intellectual training and my sensitising myself to exquisite impressions been, if I am to be killed or crippled in a month or two?* To myself in this mood I pointed out the value of my former life quite apart from its effects, insisted on the imperishability of those years, imperishable even

if nothing succeeded them, just as much as if a
well-filled half century should come after them;
and turning the thought round a little I could
say: *What does it all matter after all? It was good,
and would always have been good. You could not
have improved those years now had you lived; what,
moreover, does one life like yours matter; your good
life before this was under the hand of some
almighty power whose actions didn't refer
themselves to you, and so will it be with your death
now, or your survival.*

Occasionally, again, I thought of it from the
point of view of a full and happy youth suddenly
closed before Time could spoil it. The fear that a
useless and ugly middle-age might succeed my
youth made me glad of death. I saw, though,
even then, that this state of mind was more
suitable to epitaphs on children's tombstones
than to the reflections of a young man out a-
soldiering: and I never really thought that I
would find myself unequal to the test of maturer
life, or that I should end in failure or monotony.
The very blackst moments that I did sometimes
go through, as at B....., I have noted above, and
they came again now and then: moments when
all existence seemed futile, and even life in peace-

32

time appeared vacant and stalely useless; when all books seemed to have been written, all pictures painted, all experience and sensation opened up for no good reason at all; when the whole world was a silly blind drift, purposeless and un-intelligible in itself and populated by people whom one did not know whether to pity more for their brief mortality or to hate for their folly.

There was nothing here though that I had not felt at Oxford or Highgate before war was thought of, it was a restless state, when one's soul was masterless, and not common with me.

But a desire to be alive was one that came oftener and in a far more imperious form than any acquiescence in the prospect of death ever did. Mostly, it must be admitted, it was for material joys that continuance of life seemed necessary, for the joys that would be open to me again after we were disbanded. This love of the forms of worldly things was what gave death its main ugliness, the conviction that never again, once dead, should I touch and see the shapes of material things that I had loved so keenly. A recital like Rupert Brooke's "The Great Lover" had become increasingly possible to me as my sensibilities had widened and grown more acute;

and with this, of course, went a greater reluctance than ever to leave all these things behind me, whatever abstract beauties I might win in exchange. That I should lose my books and my pictures, and no more enjoy the activities they called up, seemed less painful, for they did not savour so intensely of earth – except some of them, now and then – as did the quite material pleasures; and, moreover, it seemed that if any life were hereafter permitted it would be of a purely rational or abstract kind, more akin, that is, to literary and artistic pleasures. In short, it was the animal that hated death and clung passionately to promise of life; the soul and the mind, save when more definitely animal, did not much repine. There were instants when all the pride of my flesh and the lust of my eye rose up in all their manifestions from highest to lowest, and willed majestcally to live. Like Plato's many-headed monster, they were intensely vigorous, felt themselves supremely capable of action and sought only the opportunity.

# A LETTER FROM THE FRONT
## An Estaminet

### *Saturday*, Feb. 12th, 1916.

Dear Lad,

I had your letter this afternoon and set myself to answer it at once. We have had rather a bloody – literally – time of it. The Tab. I had met early at Woldingham was shot in the head and killed instantly one night standing next to me, and you may have observed that we lost several officers. We had an extraordinarily heavy bombardment. Also I had rather an exciting time myself with two other men on a patrol in the "no man's land" between the lines. A dangerous business, and most repulsive on account of the smells and appearance of the heaps of dead men that lie unburied there as they fell, on some attack or other, about four months ago. I found myself much as I had expected in the face of these happenings: more interested than afraid, but more careful for my own life than anxious to approve any new martial ardour. I become, I assure you, more and more cautious, though more accustomed and easy in face of the Hun.

For the moment, thank God, we are back

resting, and the certain knowledge that I shan't be killed anyhow for a day or two is most invigorating.

The spring is manifest here, in young corn, and the very air and strong winds: and even here I react to it, and find myself chanting verses of "Love in the Valley" as I did last year in Surrey. I have an odd feeling, though very insistent and uplifting to me, a feeling which I probably vainly unfold to you, of being so integrally a part of; and so thoroughly approved and intimately associated with all these evidences of spring, that Nature herself will not suffer me to be killed, but will preserve unharmed a lover so loyal and keen-sighted as myself. We shall see.

I got a "Spenser" from T....., and am now travelling through "The Faerie Queen" with the chaste Britomart.

Yes, by all means send me "Tom Jones": those long things I can manage very well here, when we are back from the hellish trenches, where I find it hard to read, though I can manage to write letters, more or less.

I believe I shall get leave – if I am not killed or wounded first – certainly in two months' time, and possibly before. It is bruited about that the

Battalion starts leave in a day or two. My God! what heaven it will be while it lasts, and what awful hell going back!

However, I live so utterly in the moment that I can easily shelve the last few hours till they come. I hope it arrives when the spring is farther on. I will bear witness to all I can to keep you out of the Army; I am so intensely pleased that you've not got forced in yet, and I hope you will still escape. How bloody people seem to be in England about peace and peace meetings. I suppose they are getting rather Prussian in the country, but are all peace meetings always broken up by soldiers (who've probably never been there at all)?

I have contracted hatred and enmity for nobody out here, save soldiers generally and a few N.C.O.'s in particular. For the Hun I feel nothing but a spirit of amiable fraternity that the poor man has to sit just like us and do all the horrible and useless things that we do, when he might be at home with his wife or his books, as he preferred. Well, well; who is going to have the sense to begin talking of peace? We're stuck here until our respective Governments have the sense to do it.

Send me "Tom Jones" then, if you please.
I must really stop, dear lad.

A G W.

# Part Two – Diary

*Towards the end of March 1916 West came home, and was sent to train in Scotland with a view to taking a commission.*

*Part II describes his experiences during training.*

## DRILL

### *Wednesday*, April 19th, 1916.

Drill! When we first came we had done a 140 to the minute step, but this slacked off, until to-day the instructors were called before the Adjutant and told to insist on it. We marched up and down at this rate, saluting, most of the early morning.

Before brekker the Company Sergeant-Major made another speech: *That we had better work with him, it would be better for us to help him and then he could help us. This 140 was to be kept to – B.E.F. men as well. He knew we had been out there where conditions were entirely different, but we must now pull ourselves together. As regards saluting with the rifle, there had been some dispute about it. He had told us to make no noise on it, but Captain R..... had decided a noise was to be made, though where he had been for the last eighteen months the custom had been different. He saw a man smiling there among the B.E.F. men – a lance-corporal, too. Perhaps he thought himself very knowing: let him come and take over his job and see if he would laugh then. Let the Company get the name of a smart Company. The squad he himself had been taking that morning had got praised, he hadn't taken the B.E.F. men recently, and didn't know what they were like. Let them now dismiss, saluting smartly as if an officer were on parade.* At brekker we agreed that we would commit suicide if it went on; that C..... was middle-aged, being thirty-one; that happiness was never attainable (questioned).

### *Easter Monday*, April 24th, 1916.

There were to be no parades to-day. During the morning, however, we were routed out of the reading-room to put half-bricks round the front of all the huts in our line; there were ten huts.

## LEAVE

### *Wednesday*, April 26th, 1916.

We are kept in suspense about our leave; meanwhile all of us are saving thirty-five shillings for supposed fares to London, which we might otherwise spend, and are going very short.

Parade before brekker by six new sergeants,

who were tested on us by the Company Sergeant-Major. We were kept at it an hour by these men at a great pace, with no more than two minutes "easy."

Rifle exercises as usual in the morning. We were granted leave at twenty minutes' notice from Wednesday till Monday morning. Many of us had not enough money to do it, never having had notice to save money for leave. We were first told that we need not go on afternoon parade, and then were put on it for one and a-half hours.

## MORE DRILL

### *Wednesday*, May 5th, 1916.

As usual. Platoon drill under a man who didn't know the difference between column and line. A sergeant who, by his own confession, had never handled a short rifle was put on to instruct us in musketry.

We had a lecture on behaviour – *i.e., Not to go into pubs.; this could be done in France, where officers and men were not sharply distinguished; we were not to go about with obvious tarts, nor get drunk. We could, however, do all these things if we would get into mufti* – the usual assumption that all civilians somehow fall short of gentility.

In the evening we were put to scrub out huts for D Company, and arrange the beds. Nothing of the sort was done for us when we came. Some of the A Company sergeants made a protest about our having too much dirty work and no time for reading.

More musketry from the same sergeant, who knew neither the right orders nor drill-book method of instructions. Asked by Captain R..... if he had given us a target, he said "Yes, the field in front!" This fined itself down to a telegraph-post that he had never really given us at all!

## LECTURE ON DISCIPLINE

*Friday*, May 12th, 1916.

A lecture by C.O., an Englishman, rather episcopalian; a dull and studiously and coolly brutal man. Usual lines! *Discipline consists of little things. Present standard of officers considered too low; we should be the first products of the new methods. We would be faced with a very difficult problem when commissioned; being ourselves junior officers we should be expected to combat the slackness we should be sure to find there. All over England the lack of discipline was spreading; men were not saluting properly; things were going to the dogs. Discipline was a habit, a habit of the mind, not to be picked up as Territorials tried to on Saturday afternoons. The Germans, though we sneered at them at the time, were now proved to have perfected the system of training men in a short time; we must copy the Prussian method: that was what we were to expect for ourselves and to enforce on our men. He proceeded to draw contrasts between the undisciplined Anzacs and the 29th Division at the Dardanelles.*

*What we must aim at was, as he had said, the discipline of the Germans. They had got men to go again and again to the attack without wavering; that must be our ideal.* Usual clap-trap about behaviour now we wore the white band round our hats. *They would watch us here in camp, but not on leave, or at home; we must behave there as we would in camp. He impressed on us the shortness of our time and the necessity for hard work on parade and in our leisure. It must be said of us when we got to our battalions: "This is a smart officer, he knows his job." That is what they would try and teach us.*

Practice in sloping arms during the afternoon, and cleaning out huts; handles of mops to be scoured white. A Company beat us in no way so much as in the polish of their stove-backs. Orders came at noon that buttons were to be cleaned before each parade.

## DISCIPLINE

### *Saturday*, May 13th, 1916.

Early morning parade occurred with saluting with canes for an hour; various new stunts introduced. Speech by Company Sergeant-Major to the effect that if our kits, caps, and huts were not clean and correct we needn't think we would go on leave, because we wouldn't; we would stay and clean them.

Rifle inspection. Several men were had up for moving on parade, among them C..... for scratching his chin. They were brought up before Captain R....., who asked if they had any excuse. They hadn't, and he told them about discipline, about disciplined troops always beating undisciplined, of how the new officers were all found totally unable to stand still on

48

parade, how if they had been guardsmen they would be made to stand before a clock for an hour, that *they* had to stand still without moving an eyelash and were cursed for moving their eyes.

The C.O. inspected us in the huts with about ten people oozing after him. Cursed a few men for long hair or hat-band not properly white; no more said. Afterwards C.S.M. had us all on parade, said men were not to be on C.O.'s parade again with dirty boots, that overcoat buttons were to be clean, and all clean in respect of kit and equipment. Then he went on with a long rigmarole about men from Territorial Force units, and some formal filling up of papers. This lasted twenty minutes, during which time he had us at attention or at ease the whole time, never easy. Finally he did nothing with the B.E.F. men at all, and we need really never have been brought out there. The C.O. to-day ordered all the spittoons to be removed from the canteen because of the look they gave to the place; the canteen-man had paid eighteen shillings for them. We learnt, about now that the Battalion being full the course would now start in earnest and we might look forward to another four months; we might really have been away all the time.

## HOSPITAL

### *Monday*, May 15th, 1916.

S..... came back from hospital and reported cold food served after our dinner was over. Also when he was admitted to hospital he had to lie on the floor for the morning and afternoon, though many beds were vacant, because it was not known whether he had officially been admitted or not. We laid turf all the early-morning parade.

## THE OTHERS

### *Saturday*, May 20th, 1916.

Depression is merely a passing mood with the most of men, and comes rarely even so. The men with me felt indignant when told to go on a parade they didn't like, and for a moment after coming off it retained their resentment; but it soon passed off, and depression of spirits from general greyness of outlook, as an enduring attitude, was unknown to them.

The prospect of four days' leave made them all delirious; so did week-ends, or even the Wednesday half-holiday.

In the evening when work was done, the gramophone, golf, girls, a meal at a hotel, a magazine story, a piano, made them forget that they had ever had a complaint in the world, or that to-morrow would begin, as usual, with an Adjutant's parade at 5.30. C.....'s disgust was more demonstrative than E.....'s, and it amused them immensely. It was quite real, but they thought his humour was exercised for its own sake: they never came near to understanding E.....'s nature. As before, nobody could make out C....., thought he was writing an incredibly extended diary when he made his notes, but loved him for his oddity and wit; so they failed over E....., who didn't even amuse them by being quaint or publicly witty, for he was rarely this.

They are utterly commonplace people here, most of them: noisy, too, with the conventional desires and lusts.

They go to church, a lot of them, on Sundays, partly, I think, because they like the service out of religious sentimentality, partly out of custom, partly to feel themselves a part of normal civilisation again, partly to get off with a choir-girl.

## DEPRESSION

### *Friday*, May 12th, 1916.

A fearful sense of the grimness of things came over me last night, which it would have been hard to express in words even then, and of which it is hard now to recapture even the details. I had a fearful cold that grew worse and worse, and I expected that by the morning, having done guard from eleven to one, I might be really ill. E..... had just come in and told me C..... was bad; he himself didn't look well.

I knew how many of us did not feel fit here: this, combined with the stupidity of parading us for platoon drill or even physical drill in the wind and wet (we were sometimes kept an hour drilling in the pouring rain), and the ever-increasing viciousness and malice of the Adjutant and C.S.M. towards us, seemed to keep an almost personal fiend of terror hovering above our heads. The war and the Army had never looked so grim. The Army is really the most anti-social body imaginable. It maintains itself on the selfishness and hostility of nations, and in its own ranks holds together by a bond of fear and suspicion, all anti-social feeling. Men are taught to fear their superiors, and they suspect the men. Hatred must be often present, and only fear prevents it flaming out.

My feeling of impotent horror, as of a creature caught by the proprietors of some travelling circus and forced with formal brutality to go through meaningless tricks, was immensely sharpened by a charcoal drawing of C.....'s called "We Want More Men!" showing Death, with the English staff cap on and a ragged tunic, standing with a jagged sickle among a pile of bleeding, writhing bodies and smoking corpses – a huge gaunt figure that haunted me horribly.


## ARMY INSTRUCTORS

### *Thursday*, May 18th, 1916.

A hot day. We did fire-control all the time under the Adjutant, Brigade Officer, &c. One noted, first, their utter inability to teach us anything because there were too many superannuated old martinets trying to do it at the same time; secondly, the lack of doctrine among them all: even if they could have taught, they knew nothing. The way we were taught

musketry was laughable. The whole Company
was kept in close order, écheloned in half-
companies at twenty paces, and moved up and
down the field first in single rank, then in
ordinary close formation, finally halted in
échelon, and given fire-orders by the Platoon
Commander and Sectional Commanders, with
front rank kneeling, rear rank standing; the C.O.
meanwhile stood in the background for a long
time, checking people in a peevish ineffectual
way for minor irrelevances. It was always the
same thing with us; we had three men shouting
at us at once when we were on parade, each one
eager to outshine the others in his keenness in
detecting faults and the strength and accuracy of
his denunciation of the offender. It was always
impossible to please them all, and when one had
you alone he was sure to scold you for methods
on which the others had been fondly insistent.
Our instructors, and even our officers, were not
above confessing that they didn't know the drill
which they were supposed to be there to teach us.

## SWEATING THE WAITERS

### *Monday*, May 22nd, 1916.

About this time men were beginning to go up and ask to be sent back to their units. We were told when we came here that those who wished to return might do so, but this was now refused. "Men had to go on with the course." We came off guard this morning and were put on a fatigue at once by the C.S.M. to move bedding, &c., from a neighbouring hut. At eleven we had a lecture from a tired, bored young man, who leant up against the wall and read in a low, weary, indistinct voice straight out of "Field Engineering," too fast for us to take anything down, even if we wished to, not even trying to conceal the fact that none of his remarks were original. He chose, too, paragraphs of vague generalities or technical details about numbers of picks and shovels, and the amount of cubic feet a man should excavate.

The waiters who attend us at meals are at work every day, including Sundays, from 5.30 till 8.30, on their feet the whole time, one waiter to a table of twelve men, and early morning tea and biscuits, brekker, dinner, tea – often with some meat – and supper. They get only the usual shilling per diem. One is glad to see they have struck for shorter hours and less work. It was said to-day by one of the Scotch corporals, a man who had made a singularly inefficient Orderly Sergeant, that the duties of Orderly Sergeant and Orderly Corporal must be explained to the X..... men, but needn't be explained to the Scotchmen, as they knew all about it.

## A LECTURE ON MAPS

*Tuesday*, May 23rd, 1916.

Adj.'s Morning Parade was very cold. We did sizing drill and dressing all the hour: utterly useless. C.S.M. was standing about and saying he had seen recruits with two days' training do it better than we did.

Lecture by S..... on maps. A sand model had been erected on a table by this person, which occupied him an hour in the morning. He had put tapes and flags on it to signify contours and heights, and explained the features at enormous length: of course we all knew them and realised it was all eye-wash. He showed that he didn't know the difference between concave and convex, and bungled away for twenty minutes before a blackboard on which he had drawn an abominably bad map.

## MEALS

*Undated.*

Communication drill in the afternoon, bawling across to one another in the old absurd way.

Alteration in meals. The food both degenerates and diminishes; meat baked to a dry cinder, and not enough of it comes on at lunch; pudding of any sort seems to be knocked off entirely; cheese, jam, &c., are not provided at all as they used to be. Tea to-day at 4.30 consisted simply of a few cakes and tea; we shall see what supper is. The food as it is now would not be so bad were it not that we were led to expect something very different from our first weeks here. I suspect it has worked out as follows. The allowance for our food is very generous, and it must have been pretty well spent out at first: obviously it would be better if our food should be reduced to the ordinary Army minimum and the surplus should go elsewhere. A convenient way of doing this presented itself when the staff of waiters sent in a complaint that their work was too heavy and they got no leisure. We were told that on their account we were to have supper and tea knocked together at six. We all agreed to this. It does not look as if it would be done. For this modified tea and supper does not relieve the waiters at all, and the C.O. told them when a deputation was sent up to him that it was all nonsense to expect leisure nowadays, they must go on working the usual hours. Thus they keep the staff in their places, manage to reduce the expense of feeding us, and gain the money for themselves under the pretence of lessening the waiters work, and neither we nor the staff reap any profit.

The C.S.M. "asked" us to pick up the loose stones about the lines. He said, with his vulpine grin, that he would ask us, he would not order out a fatigue for it. After tea the whole Company was ordered out to do the job.

Supper to-night consisted of jugs of water, no hot cocoa as before, bread, butter, jam, and some tinned fish in a plate. No waiters were about at all.

# THE COMPANY SERGEANT-MAJOR

## *Wednesday*, May 24th, 1916.

C.S.M. horribly prolix to-day. After Adj.'s Parade we heard A Company being dismissed, and we were kept on to have orders read to us and to have a speech thrown in: *That we were very slack in turning out of the 'uts; when he blew his whistle down the lines he saw men standing with their heads round the door of the 'uts. Then, when we were called for by him we must come at once, quick time, preferably double. Men went along now at slow time. We never saw him come up to an officer in slow time, he went at the double, and what was good enough for him was good enough for us.*

Several men were had up for laughing and talking during this speech, including G..... for about the tenth time, as C.S.M. only knows his name.

By the new regulations the net is drawn closer. South Beach Hotel in T..... is now out of bound. The C.O. lives there and finds us troublesome, we think. At the same time we have been forbidden to drink at pubs. The only other hotel in T..... is a Temperance one, and hence we cannot have any drinks there at all. Liberty of wearing private kit, even away from camp, is taken from us. This was allowed even in the M..... Regiment.

We went a route march this morning and got back very late. More degeneration of food, measly tasteless apples.

## THE BOOK OF SIN

### *Thursday*, May 25th, 1916.

Morning parade prefaced by a dispute between C..... and the C.S.M., because the bugler had sounded all the calls very late, and the C.S.M. first objected to our turning out without regard to the bugle, and then cursed us for not being ready.

C.S.M. sneered, and kept saying: "*Be a soldierlike thing to do to show up the bugler – very soldierlike, wouldn't it? Very soldierlike thing to do.*"

The morning parade itself was the most comic we have ever had, if it were not all so pitiable. We abandoned yesterday's marching on markers by platoons, which was some faint use for Battalion ceremonial. C.S.M. tried to explain, in a muddle of words that would have perplexed Wisdom herself, the ways of throwing out markers. Then the Adjutant came up and amended and contradicted his explanation, and the C.S.M., who understood not a tittle of it all, stood in the rear clutching nervously at his stick, pawing at his more salient features, and ticking us all off for absurd little faults merely to show he was awake. We moved vaguely about on lines of markers, were dressed and re-dressed by left, right, and centre, first by one then by another, and then by a third. The authorities rushed foaming and heated up and down the ranks, pushing and thrusting men about, bawling and gesticulating like three peevish little boys playing with lead soldiers, and all wanting to do something different with them. Long lists of positions and regulations for Battalion ceremonial and Company ceremonial drill were reeled off at us in angry vulgar Scotch by the Adjutant, and we were expected to comprehend all at once.

The C.S.M. was most awful to-day in his speeches. He had the sick up before him at eleven o'clock, and told several of them off for malingering, and then laid down the rule that *all sick men were to parade before every Company parade.*

The afternoon is black with sin. Before parade the C.S.M. and an officer, D....., came round every platoon examining the hair and telling men off all round.

No camp barber is supplied, or if he is, is never there. Many names were taken. Then we marched off and were taken by the Adjutant in ceremonial drill. This was like the morning, only worse. A roaring wind made it impossible to hear any commands, and what use it is all meant to be, God only knows. The C.O. hung about dubiously round the edges of the company, looking at his feet and striking attitudes with his stick, finally slouching off without a word. Then some of us fired five rounds at the miniature range. Before we went there we were closed up for a speech in the lines, by the C.S.M. It was admonitory, confidential, and anecdotal:

*Some of you men, 'ave been to the Front, and you've got a bit 'eavy – very 'eavy you've got, some of you. Well, you've been 'ere seven or eight weeks now and you ought to begin to shape a bit. You've 'ad lots of warning; I 'ad no warning when I joined the servace. I recollect when I didn't turn my 'ead and eyes, the Colour Sergeant 'e comes up to me and taps me on the shoulder and says: "Your name, and next I knew was I 'ad four hours' pack-drill – four hours I 'ad straight off the reel. Then about this 'air-cut. I remember in my squad when I was in the service, a lad came on with long 'air, and the officer told 'im off to 'ave 'is 'air cut; 'e came on the afternoon parade with 'is 'air not cut; 'e was brought up and 'ad seven days' cells; seven days' cells 'e 'ad. I knows you, some of you; you take on sullen; you take and cut about coming on parade early; well, I say to them men "Come and fall in a company 150 strong yourself, and march it down to hadutant's parade – inspect it, and march down to hadjutant's parade all in a quarter of a hour." We know the men that comes out sullen, that means to get through with as little work as they can, that are 'ere to 'ave a good time in their certain limitations.*

He then passed on to strictures on boots, hair, buttons, and equipment: *That we should be had up before the C.O. for the next offence and should find ourselves back with our units. If we wanted to go back we should say so, they would send us back; they didn't want the trouble of training us: it was our own fault if we didn't all go away with commissions. We must all fall into line, speaking to us as a man to men* (we all shuddered at that). *He said that we ought to do this, we ought to do our best.* Noticeable through this, as through all speeches and exhortations that were ever made to us, was the insistence that we should do our best, and no hint of a fulfilment of the contract towards us. Three officers, we hear, were listening to the C.S.M.'s speech and laughing at it.

In the evening C..... was sent for by C.S.M. and was with him for over an hour. It turned out that C.S.M., who is called W....., is a man I had met. At Oxford he was a clerk in the P.O., and J..... and I had some correspondence and an interview with him over some social meeting. He was in his letters and speech just such a prolix vain weakling as he is now, and I can recall his leering squint round the door, his curled-back lips, glistening possibly false teeth, and his eyes so narrow and slit-like that they seemed almost deformed. In the interview with C..... it came out that C.S.M. was ground down by the officers, bullied by the sergeants. *"Look at my 'at,"* he said to C....., *"you may not believe it, but it's the only one of the sort in the mess."* He hates the officers, of whom it now appears that the Adjutant has never been at the Front, and even our Major at the beginning was only a Terrier. He sees the absurdity of the training, expected, as we did, to be put at Oxford, has a wife and children very badly off (the Sergeants' mess get no messing allowance, and have to keep it up out of their own pay). He said it was the C.O. who cut down our food, having been assured by the doctor that we were eating too much and going sick because of it. The waiters' evil condition he corroborated, many were back wounded from France, and got only one pass in nine weeks. They could get no redress from the C.O. On the score that we, when we became officers, would be able to lead a slack life, he urged us to become fit for commissions. On all hands this consideration is urged on us for taking commissions. C..... put to him the old fact that bullying would do no good with men like us, it simply made us bored and indifferent, and we would not do even the work that we could do, well.

## MORE SIN

### *Friday*, May 26th, 1916.

Company drill in the morning under the C.S.M. It was very cold and we were kept standing still. Then the Adjutant came and cursed us for bad arm drill; we had hands so cold we couldn't do it. The C.S.M. made a speech in our lines after this parade: *We must do better arm drill; we 'ad a bad name already, and didn't want to get a badder.* He also gave out that the Adjutant had told him to let us know that the C.O. had been complaining again about our unsteadiness on parade, and would, if any man were brought up to him, send him back to his unit. ( *N.B.* – It appears from C.....'s last night's interview that several of us are already on the black-list and will *not* be sent back to our unit, but to the X..... depot, whence we may go to any battalion.)

It is noteworthy that the C.O. has originated no order or sentiment other than these little trivialities. The higher commands are all reducible to this (as far as concerns the men): they all have their little fads, which become practically the whole of their individuality; one is hot on buttons, another on steadiness in the ranks, another on saluting, another on blankets, another on stove-tops, &c.

Again a sinful afternoon. The C.S.M. had us out half an hour before parade; then ceremonial, the Adjutant yapping about here, there, and everywhere; hut-scrubbing, whitewashing of stones, scrubbing of bed-boards, and broom handles. Preparation hour from five to six made a wash-out in order to have us handy for the C.S.M.'s fatigues. They always knock off this hour if one has to go on fatigues, and then expect us to find time and quiet to read up and answer questions. The men made a complaint to-day at being marched in solemnly in fours to take a cup of tea and two buns. The officer said he would lodge the complaint. I learnt that many men with bad teeth were being detained at their work in camp, whatever their sufferings, until the doctor had gathered together a whole platoon to attend the dentist.

## PARADE

### *Saturday*, My 27th, 1916.

This morning we had saluting drill for half an hour. It was the most pitiably comic parade I have ever seen, even here. First we were drilled in platoons: our official way of carrying the stick was outlined, and a special drill, by numbers, drawn up, for tucking the stick under the arm, taking it into the hand again, and cocking it up in the air. We practised in two movements:

1. Put the stick under left arm;
2. Cut the right hand away; then
1. Seize stick on the under-side;
2. Bring it smartly down to the side.

We were then marched up and down the road saluting by numbers imaginary officers, thus:

1. Stick under arm;
2. Hand away;
1, 2, 3, 4, 5, put hand up;
6. Hand down;
1. Hand up to stick again;
2. Hand and stick away.

We did this for a quarter of an hour, yelling out the numbers. On all hands were other platoons rushing about in the same way. After this, when it had been impressed on us how hot the C.O. was on saluting and looking officers straight in the eyes, "like a soldier, as man to man, not gazing into distant regions," we were formed up, both Companies A and B, in fours. Then about twenty men were put out in a wide circle with a diameter of about two hundred yards, and the whole two companies were marched round this circle. Each four went off separately at intervals of a few paces, saluting the twenty men on the circumference of the circle as they came to each of them. There were about seventy lots of fours going round like this, the Adjutant, the C.S.M., and A and B Companies' C.S.M.'s standing about in the middle of the circle like circus managers. For a quarter of an hour the procession went ceaselessly round, each four making the tour three times, and then we were closed and marched in home.

Physical drill came immediately after brekker, and violent running, jumping, and abdominal exercises. The day was very hot.

There were two mildly revolutionary drawings of C.....'s in the hut for C.O.'s inspection to-day: a bloated General on inspection, and a satirical cartoon of a man in the 10th Battalion in a motley dress, half-man half-officer, fettered by red tape and chains and stamped with broad arrows.

The C.S.M. formed us up for a speech this morning as usual, and read a letter to us from the C.O., not addressed to us, but concerning us. It desired *that the cadets be informed that very little improvement in steadiness in the ranks had been noticed; that men talked and moved on parade, that a system of punishment was being devised to meet the case, and deprivation of all week-ends would be the probable punishment. Every cadet found guilty of this offence would be personally interviewed by the C.O. and dealt with according to his offence.* Then he went on to say, he dared say that many of us detested the Army and had been doing so since the first day the war started. He assured us that he did the same thing, but yet would do everything he was told, and perform any duty however disagreeable; we must all do out best and fall into line.

## ETHICAL CREED

*Undated.*

I believe that I am getting more perfectly to the state of Stoicism to which I aspire. I do really care less than I used to do for the fools and bullies in command of me. They certainly do not frighten me at all as they used to. I don't care a jot for the Adjutant or the C.O. when they come and yap or make heavy speeches at me. I do not mind if I am ticked off on parade, and I don't think I should be at all shamed if I were finally turned down altogether. And they do not bore me as much as they do some people like C.....; I can throw off the mask of attention that I put on my mind perforce on parade, as soon as I come off it. C..... bears it very badly. But I am approaching more nearly to E.....'s state of mind, I think; I mean a state of Nihilism rather than of Stoicism. For Stoicism's fundamental assumption was the positive one that only the good is good, and for that we should live; whereas I sometimes think rather that nothing is good or has any permanent value whatever.

I noted it down some weeks ago that pessimism, by which I must practically have meant Nihilism, was all very well as a pose, but paralysed action for good or effort towards happiness.

But now I see the great attractiveness and mournful pleasure of the creed that nothing is. Moods of this kind have overcome me utterly some days lately; and I have understood the feelings of poets when they have written of the vanity of things and the nothingness of all earthly importances. One is apt to let such utterances go by as merely conventional, beautiful expressions of a sentiment to which people gladly accede in verse, but which they do not really credit for a moment in daily thought and action: and would think a man mad for carrying such beliefs into practical existence. Perhaps such poems are often shallow, the outcome of some personal disappointment, when a man, robbed of his dearest wish, unjustly conceives that all wishes, both his own and other peoples, are necessarily vain and fore-doomed to see no fruition. And yet many men must have felt this in the general impersonal sense, while life and hope remained to them and they still took keen pleasure in the play of thought and feeling.

I have realised this for myself – the absolute

nonentity of everything that men hold precious. Even the decision of this war is nothing; what does England matter, or whether she wins or not? Any man of sense must subscribe with all his mind and soul to the cry of Ecclesiastes; when he goes to the British Museum and sees the meaningless lost-looking Thoths and Rameses, Sphinxes and mummies, he must feel that they are now nothing; when he thinks of the wars whose voice has come ever so faintly down to us from those ages, and of all the men and women of those times, he must understand that all existence from the earliest Egyptian dynasties and æons before them, to the present day, and on and on into the future, is without meaning, of no absolute or continuous importance. Mankind is perpetually puffing itself up with strange unearthly loyalties and promised rewards. Man goes out to fight for a delusion, to defend what he has tricked up as his Fatherland; he imposes all sorts of restraints and tortures on himself in the name of Virtue and Respectability, sets a fool above him to worship, crawl on his knees to, and shed a blessing of "purposefulness" on his most frightful sufferings.

There is only one thing real amidst all this

decorative garbage, and that is the feeling of pain or pleasure, together with thought. To bring happiness into the world is the only aim of action; action undertaken for any other motive is wasted. We may seek the happiness of ourselves and of others. The existence of happiness and pain, with certain means of attaining them, is the fundamental reality on which I would now base any scheme of life I were to construct. It is true that I get happiness from being with my friends, from reading and writing, therefore I do it and can justify myself in doing it; it is true that I bring happiness to my parents by doing and suffering things which, while they do me no harm, please them. But all other creations that are supposed to have a claim on my time and life I spurn. I spurn the idea that I am naturally enthusiastic for the success of my hut or Platoon or Company or Battalion; that I am necessarily fonder of my own country than any other, and most of all, now, I reject the presumption that I worship a God by Whose never-wronging hand I conceive all the present woe to have keen brought upon the now-living generation of mankind. If there is a God at all responsible for governing the earth, I hate and abominate Him

– I rather despise Him. But I do not think there is one. We only fall into the habit of calling down curses on a god whom we believe not to exist, because the constant references to his beneficence are so maddening that anger stings us to a retort that is really illogical.

## THE GLASGOW ART GALLERY

### *Sunday*, May 28th, 1916.

I went to the Glasgow Art Gallery in the warm glowing afternoon with C..... and T..... Many pictures had been removed for safety, such as Whistler's "Carlyle." Still, we saw much that was beautiful. Especially some of J. Maris, Anton Mauve, Boilers, and Bosboom.

They paint chiefly in water-colour. Maris had two exquisite little pictures, one of his two children, and one of a girl asleep on a sofa, full of a lively and intimate charm.

Two more good pictures were Clausen's "Portrait of a Girl in Black" and Homell's "Children Gathering Snowdrops."

There is some very good Corot there, and Lavery and Orchardson. Coming out of the gallery, on the steps above the level of Kelvingrove Park, looking down the broad paths, on one side of which crept a slow river, whose banks were buried in thick clumps of bushy trees, I felt that I was regarding not reality but one of the Dutch pictures of Prius or Ostade, or Canaletto's canals and wide prospects in Italian cities.

There seemed a kind of film in the air which gave to the scene the semblance of a painting, already feeling the hand of Time, and separating it, as by a pane of glass, from the beholder, rendering it remote and not a creation of the passing day. In the background were high piled grey-white clouds, above which an indeterminate milky blue intensified into a deep azure: spires and towers sprang up behind the large solid blocks of building, very Dutch in character, that skirted the confines of the park.

From where we stood the movement of the people up and down the paths was so little apparent that they helped rather than hindered the illusion of a picturesque unreality. Give them more colour in dress, more generous splendour of gait and gesture, and they would have satisfied Prius or Canaletto.

As we came down among them the illusion vanished and the town took back its power. But still, here and there presented itself a scene so essentially paintable that it received, despite its momentary mutability and decay, something of the eternal rest and life of an emotion set for all time in colour or words. Life is at times so gorgeous, so full of beauties, from the deafening blare of stormcrowned sunsets to the miniature daintinesses of a butterfly's wing – and mankind contributes his share, in the beauty of his body and the beauty of his art and song – that I could lie down and cry that it should be thrown into a world so empty and planless. I ought not to modify this determination to regard existence here as vanity: indeed It supplies more evidence still for the contention: it is but another clue of thread put into our hand in this minotaur's labyrinth, promising to lead us out to realms of order and delight; whereas from this maze there is no escape for living man.

## THE NORTH SEA AFFAIR

*Friday*, June 3rd, 1916.

The serious defeat of the Fleet in the North Sea – as we believe it to be – has produced little effect in most men who talked loudly of national honour and prestige. They rushed to buy papers this morning in haste to find out what had happened, laughed scornfully at the Navy's anticlimax, remarked that it was on the Army, and Kitchener's Army at that, on which we had to depend: and then they seemed to forget all about it. The news, or rather its confirmation, brought C..... to a state of very bad temper, which worked itself off in swearing at the orderly, and then jokes in the hut.

It is in face of such a calamity, so stunning in its sudden impact, and forming such an ironic background to the dance of mankind, that I am rejoiced at my sense of nothingness and utter lack of importance.

## A SPECIAL LECTURE

### *Thursday*, June 16th, 1916.

A lecture by a cavalry major who is a physical-drill expert. For his arrival we had to wear our little thin vests and bags instead of our shirts and trousers. We had formerly given these in, but they were brought out to-day. The whole Battalion was paraded at twelve, and the Major, a small man with an incredibly evil countenance, and a soft hat on one side – a jaunty man and with an inability to pronounce his R's – gave a lecture on physical drill and bayonet fighting. Points:

*Physical drill to be done in the trenches! It often could be done even under shell-fire. Never let a man off! Punish him for all offences, even the slightest. His pals'll chip him and he'll pull together.* (Note total lack of comprehension of ordinary man's psychology; in an army where all the ranks were criminals or seducers and the officers all bloody bullies the regiment could only be kept up like this; nowadays such treatment engenders sheer hatred and makes men give the smallest they can without being caught; treated like gentlemen they would give all they could.) *Story of officer whom nobody disobeyed twice. Someone disobeyed him once and he went to the hospital! Cheers!*

This man babbled on about bayonet fighting and physical drill until 12.45, the C.O. simpering by, keeping a thousand men from their rest and their beer, and teaching them nothing.

## THE CASE OF N.....

*Tuesday*, July 5th, 1916.

No longer allowed to smoke in lectures. Bitterly cold, rainy and windy; yet we had to stand about in small squads on the parade-ground and do arm drill till 7.45. After brekker we went and did platoon drill, then came in, were stood in a hut and made to do arm drill by the C.S.M. He insulted us all the time and cursed us, as he always was doing just now, for being unsteady, worse than "men he had known with a fortnight in the mallishyer."

We did arm drill for forty minutes. I remark here the case of N.....: he had had an abscess in a top molar and had to go down to the dentist.

From him he had to get an estimate of the cost of treating the tooth. The dentist presented an estimate of 2/6 for cleaning out the tooth, and 2/6 for refilling it. This estimate N..... gave in to the authorities at camp and received it back a week after the day he had first gone sick with the second 2/6 crossed out – *i.e.*, the Army were willing to pay the first but not the second.

This afternoon we again did platoon drill in the drizzly cold wind. The C.S.M. seems really mad; he alternates between the most vicious martinetism and the most reckless affability; as, for instance, this afternoon, when he was unnecessarily rude to men on parade, and then on the ground asked publicly for lozenges for his throat, said *He was very pleased with us and we must work together. When we came out we were to make as good a show as he did (and that wouldn't be very much, he said); we were to be the officers, not him, he would never be an officer (cries of "Yes, yes!").*

He told us that he with our help and we with his would finally make a good show as a company.

The C.O. was on parade and seems a fool; cursed us, and kept us standing in the rain to tell us to look into his eyes when we saluted him. We were paraded for the usual five-to-six hour by C.S.M. as for a lecture, but he had made a mistake, and there was none.

## CARRYING COAL

*Friday*, July 8th, 1916.

The C.S.M. getting more unpopular. Organised "Boo's" surge up from the ranks against him on parade; they get louder and louder.

Two men per hut were told off to fetch coal for officer's mess in the afternoon, and missed parade. They will not let us off parade to do orderly work in the huts, but don't mind our coming off to carry coal for them. There were plenty of the staff who could have done it.

## GOING SICK!

*Saturday*, July 9th, 1916.

Went sick. Headache, &c. C.S.M. came in about seven and cursed me for still lying in bed, and went up and shouted at one man who had been in bed two days quite poorly. We were told to *wake up, stir up; that he had to get up when he was ill. Did we think the doctor would come and see us there? He (C. S.M) would go to the doctor as long as he could crawl to him. We were men now, not boys, and we must pull ourselves together; we should get up and begin to tidy up the hut.* About twenty minutes after he came in and cursed us all again. After brekker the sick paraded, and G..... was badly scolded for having us there late. Then we were told that *perhaps we didn't know that days when we were sick were struck off our training and had to be completed at the end; perhaps if we had known that we should not have gone sick.*

### ORDERS

*Monday*, July 11th, 1916.

A fine day with a cold wind. A parade of two Companies before brekker under the Adjutant. He explains things noisily, clumsily, inefficiently and impatiently. A man gets too nervous to speak as soon as he comes out under his eye. Physical drill after brekker. Several men scolded by instructor (acting under the orders of an officer) for coming out with cardigans on. They replied they had colds. They were told that didn't matter, that they knew what orders were and were guilty of a crime in coming out improperly clothed. Men were to go sick if they had colds. A lot of men in A Company turned round and shouted: "We aren't allowed to go sick with colds. That's orders, too!"

The officer looked uncomfortable, blushed, and was silent. The physical drill was very unpopular; we would be kept standing sometimes for a quarter of an hour in our lines waiting for the parade: in our short-sleeves, with a cold keen wind and sometimes a drizzling rain falling. To-day some of the men who had been sick yesterday – sixteen of B Company went sick that day – were still sick, and reported so. The doctor complained of the number of malingerers in the battalion, and said the Army method was to suppose a man was shamming until you found he was sick. Compare with this the explanation our doctor of the 16th Blankshire gave to C..... who was turned down for a commission on account of a bad heart and who asked for a discharge. "You can't apply for a discharge; you will be kept as a private. You see, we have to be so much more particular about examining officers because an officer when he is sick costs so much more." A Tommy when sick is either laughed or bullied down, or if it is too evident that he really is ill a cheap way is found of dealing with him. We went for a route march this morning and sang songs, among others "What shall we do with the Sergeant-Major?"

On our return, before parading for a lecture, the C.S.M. spoke at length on our unsatisfactoriness as a Company: our unsteadiness, our uncleanliness, unsmartness, unsoldierlike qualities. *We seemed to think we were in for a soft job. We weren't; we were to be treated just as soldiers, and ought to set ourselves a higher standard: unfortunately we set ourselves a lower. He had known men with three weeks' training in the malisshyer – men with a fortnight's training: yes, he'd known men with a fortnight's training stand more steady than we men did, some of us, with more than a year. We must get rid of the habits we had acquired in the field and try and be soldiers again! And finally* (this was mentioned rather more nervously at the end), *that some men in the front four ranks had been singing personal songs where names of N.C.O.'s were mentioned; that he had spoken to them of this; that we knew it was not allowed, we had all our military law books and hours for reading them up.* Loud laughter and groans, which he was bound to take more or less lightly.

Between A and B Company there was a football match this afternoon and Captain R..... said tentatively that it "would be a good thing" if those who had nothing special to do this afternoon went and watched it. Nobody found time hang heavy enough on his hands to do that. It was a half-holiday. One wonders how long Wednesdays will remain really free, how long before the mocking illusion of an afternoon's leisure being maintained, we are forced to play or attend football matches.

## SOME REMARKS ABOUT HOSPITALS

### *Thursday*, April 13th, 1916.

We were isolated for measles. Operations in hospital were performed unnecessarily – *e.g.*, C.....'s "varicose" vein operation, which was futile. Use of enema before operations: brutal injections. Regulation quantity to be given to each man irrespective of his make or condition;

misery of patients during the operations; lack of consideration shown to men about to undergo operations in the hearing of men already operated on near them, all bloody. Eye-wash for inspections: dying men made to sit up and ordered to smile. Doctor unsympathetic: looked on everyone as a shirker or, in his words, "skrimshanker." Hospital hopelessly under-staffed in orderlies and nurses. Brutality in treatment of patients when they were unwilling to undergo a certain cure, *e.g.*, electric battery: man wounded and minus an arm fought the orderlies, insisted on not being put under electricity; was knocked down and held on the bed by two men. Lack of men to attend entailed much suffering to patients confined to bed; couldn't relieve themselves without bed-pan, and nobody to bring it; people nearly crying with pain. Gloom of building, dirty bathroom: taps, *e.g.*, all loose and tied on to wall with string. Exercise-ground for walks, &c., was merely a scraggy bit of field, with no grass, bounded on one side by a high wall and on the other by a cemetery. Passes granted to patients to send to their friends; two people per man; case of man who came back from Front on short leave and rushed straight from his train to the hospital to see his brother who was there; he was refused admission, having no pass. Meals never hot, much worse even than ordinary camp food. Only servable at strictly regulated times; thus men from the trenches arriving late at night, wounded, wet and muddy, could be given no food because the next meal was not till brekker at eight in the morning. The nurses managed to heat up some cocoa left over from the last meal and gave them that.

# Part Three – Diary

§ Beginning of new views
§ The last leave § Notes written
on Box Hill Station § On change
§ Highgate § Officers and the war
§ "Why go on?" § Coming home
to London on leave

*In August 1916 West obtained a few weeks' leave preparatory to taking a Commission.*

*During this time his beliefs in general and his attitude to the war in particular underwent a profound change. The following extracts describe these changes. They contain some of the most moving writing in the whole Diary.*

## BEGINNING OF NEW VIEWS

### *Tuesday*, August 8th, 1916.

I now find myself disbelieving utterly in Christianity as a religion, or even in Christ as an actual figure. I seem to have lost in softness and become harder, more ferocious in nature, and in appearances certainly, by virtue of my moustache! So violently do I react against the conventional religion that once bound me – or if it did not bind me, at any rate loomed behind me – that I loathe and scorn all emotionalism and religious feeling. When I was at E..... waiting for a commission to come, I was boarded on two persons, with whom and their friends I had several arguments, I in favour of science and abstract truth, and they in favour of emotion, denying advance of knowledge and running down science itself as a work of the devil. Of course, more often I was simply tolerant of all this sort of thing, *e.g.*, among parsons and my family, but sometimes it burned up very fiercely; as when I found J..... was against me *re* Christ, and liked to believe he existed, simply because he was a "jolly" character. It seems to me shameful that a man with his power of mind should be regardless of Truth, should hold that the question is one that doesn't matter; whereas I, of far less able mind, have by my nature's law to struggle on after Truth with my inferior equipment. He threw cold water on the whole affair and made me for the moment the bitterer. Really, as I see now, the matter is not one of great importance, simply because belief in the efficacy of the figure is the important thing and the reality of the existence does not longer concern me.

## THE LAST LEAVE

### *Tuesday*, August 15th, 1916.

I had returned to London, and X..... and Z....., after a week with J..... and M..... at Box Hill. Asked if I had seen my name, as gazetted in the papers, I said "No, I had seen no paper since I went down to Dorking." Cries of "Graeme! seen no paper! How can you live?"

Most people are unable to see beyond the war at all; they cannot even realise that it is not the most important thing in the world, Truth and Beauty and Love being more so. How then shall they ever understand the truth that the world is an iota of the solar system, the solar system an iota of the universe, and the whole under the mindless rule of Primal force?

You can see how great a change it was to me, coming away from Box Hill and the free happy life of J..... and M..... and the baby and A..... and lovely H..... on Sundays, to the narrow society of ordinary people and to a world bounded by the columns of the *Morning Post*. I thought when I went down to Box Hill, and I was quite bound to feel so, that I should not be really happy with them: I thought their happy carelessness would annoy me, that I, would long for the company of those who had suffered as I had suffered, that the men with iron in their souls would be my only true companions from the war days onwards.

I was mistaken. The view was dictated by a self-fostered gloominess perhaps, a selfishness at finding my own fearful experiences unaccounted of. I was happy to put them by, and fell in love with all the sublime life of Reason, Art, and Joy more than ever.

I come back here to-night to find a summons to go to W..... in D..... and join up with the X..... Regiment.

As usual, the blow has quietened me. It has fallen, and now nothing can happen for a day or two.

I can barely convince myself that I am going back to the Army – that there is a war on at all.

Strong upon me to-night, with M.....'s laugh and J.....'s voice far away, is the now familiar feeling of unreality, of dream-existence.

What midgets we all are, what brief phantoms in a dream – a dream within a dream, this truly is my life, and how gladly would I end it now.

## NOTES WRITTEN
## ON BOX HILL STATION

*Saturday*, August 19th, 1916.

I have just been revisiting J..... and M.....; D..... M..... is there, too. I go to W..... on Monday. We read Wells's "Last Trump" out of "Boon" on a hill. If the war were to begin to-morrow and were to find me as I am now, I would not join the Army, and if I had the courage I would desert now. I have been reading and thinking fundamentally important things this last few months.

What right has anybody to demand of me that I should give up my chance of obtaining happiness – the only chance I have, and the only thing worth obtaining here?

Because they are foolish enough – not reasonable enough – to give their own up, that is no reason why I should abandon mine. I asked no one to form societies to help me exist. I certainly asked no one to start this war.

To help on happiness as much as possible I do not object, but I believe the best way to do it would be to incite people not to form armies or fight or be absurdly and narrowly patriotic. This feeling must be suppressed, broadened out, not encouraged.

My feelings and emotional experiences during these days were so strange and intense that I intend to register them as accurately as possible.

I had been on leave from G..... since late in July, and had grown quite into the way of civil life again among my friends, especially after a very delightful week in J.....'s cottage with M..... and the baby.

Hence I was able to view the whole war, the part I had played in it and the part I was destined to play in the future, from a standpoint to which

I had never been able to attain since the war began or I enlisted.

The thought of returning to the Army was, as I have said, so awful, that the knowledge that it was perpetually hanging over my head made the days seem dreamlike, merely the prelude to the time when the dream should develop into the intense horror of a nightmare.

I read a good deal of liberal literature, met some conscientious objectors, moved much among men not at all occupied in the war, and hence suffered a violent revulsion from my old imagined glories and delights of the Army (such as I had had) – its companionship, suffering courageously and of noble necessity undergone – to intense hatred of the war spirit and the country generally.

Most particularly Bertrand Russell's "Justice in War Time" impressed me, especially because his essay on the "Free Man's Worship" so delighted me as the only quite true and nobly open-minded account of a possible religion.

I so loathed the idea of rejoining the Army that I determined to desert and hide away somewhere.

This was so strong with me on Saturday,

August 19th, when, rather against my family's wishes, I went down to J..... for the last time. Never was the desire to desert and to commit suicide so overwhelming, and had it not been that I knew I would pain many people, I would certainly have killed myself that night. I imagined myself getting a knife, putting its point carefully between two ribs, and driving it home with the intensest pleasure and no feeling for the pain.

On that evening I stayed up late and read B. Russell's "Justice in War Time," and went to bed so impressed with its force that I determined to stand out openly against re-entering the Army. I was full of a quiet strong belief and almost knowledge that I should not, after all, have to face the trial of entering a new regiment as an officer, and that Waterloo would not see me at 2.10 to go to W.....

In the morning I was still determined. I didn't go to church when asked to do so, but re-read B. Russell, and made up my mind to announce to the family at lunchtime that "I have come to a serious decision, long thought out, and now morally determined on. It will influence me more than you, and yet perhaps you ought to know of it. I am not going to rejoin the Army. There is no object, except the gratification of a senseless rivalry, in prolonging the struggle; it is beastly and degrading. Why do we go on fighting? I will not go on."

I really nearly did say it. Everybody thought me silent and depressed because I was returning to the Army. It was not so. However, I said nothing. I walked down to the tram with X..... and Y....., and said nothing. And I returned, read "Boon" to Z....., and after much thought wrote to the Adjutant of the Battalion telling him I would not rejoin the Army nor accept any form of alternative service, that I would rather be shot than do so, and that I left my name and address with him to act as he pleased.

Shortly after midnight I went down to the post with this letter and two more, one to J....., one to E....., telling them what I had done. I stood opposite the pillar-box for some minutes wondering whether I would post them – then put them in my pocket and returned home to bed.

Next morning my aversion was as great and my determination not to rejoin as strong as ever. This was Monday morning, the day I had telegraphed I would rejoin. I thought I would tell the remainder of the family, Z..... and the maids. I didn't. I got furiously into my new uniform and went off after brekker to cash a cheque and get my hair cut and order a cab. As the barber cut my hair I determined I would go down and telegraph that I could not come to W....., and that explanations were following. I walked to a telegraph-office to do so – and bought two penny stamps and walked out again. I cashed a cheque for £10, saying in excuse that it might help me if I determined to desert.' Then I went to order a cab, but thought at the last moment I would walk on to a telegraph office beyond the cab office. I turned back soon after I had passed the office and ordered the cab. This settled it, I thought.

I returned home, packed, wrote to J....., had lunch, and half-communicated my state of mind to Z....., without letting her see how near I had come to fulfilling it. Then I read her some Bertrand Russell, and shocked her sentiments a good deal by what I said. I departed in a state of cynical wrath against myself and the world in general, who would understand so little of what I meant. At Waterloo I met E....., who had been sent to Woolwich in mistake for W..... Seeing him so encouraged me that I forgot my woes for a bit.

As we drew near W....., horror of rejoining the Army was making me very miserable; moreover, I had been reading B. R. in the train, and was encouraged to believe that – as I put it to myself – I might yet quite succeed in keeping my mind and spirit straight, even if I could not induce myself to acknowledge it among my enemies and those who would be indifferent to me. I said to E..... that I had come to think so differently now that I would not rejoin the Army were the war to begin, as it were, to-morrow, and that if I had the pluck I would desert now. I said I was under so many delusions when I joined at first; most of these had faded, especially religious ones. I had seen how utterly wide of Truth most of mankind – even accredited professors, &c. – were in this matter, and thus was quite prepared to find them wrong about war in general and this war in particular. I found them fully as wrong as I expected, and was only anxious to dissociate myself from them in thought, if I daren't in action.

E..... rather sniffed at the idea: said that we

could not have done anything different at the time, and that we would do the same again under like circumstances: that having discovered new truth made, or would make, any difference to his actions, he denied. But I feel that I would not do the same thing again.

## ON CHANGE
### A Free Man's Worship

*Thursday*, August 24th, 1916.

It is at least possible, owing to the wild caprice of mood and emotion, which yet do seem to advance definitely on some line or other – do not, I mean, throw down one set of values simply to rebuild it later, but build quite anew on what they ruin – it seems possible, having regard to this, that my whole outlook on life will change so utterly again that I shall barely know myself. So deep have the changes in me been recently through Christianity, Theism, Paganism, to Atheism and Pessimism, and so rapidly have they consummated themselves, that I seemed till only a few weeks ago an entirely new being. And even now I think those changes were greater and more lasting than any I have ever undergone until now. But yet I see them now as still part of a system: they, too, share the general flame-like character of man's life in that, though their blaze was high and searing, yet they pass, and the continuous fire of my existence goes on under different aspects. I have not been by them utterly consumed, still it is true πάντα ρεî and here, too, will come a change, a great change perhaps. I had regarded them as something too utterly final, I was wrong. The tendency to seek for finality, to look for some resting-place in development, some road offering shelter more permanent than nightly inns is a delusion, and not to be acquiesced in. Still the change goes on and still I travel forward.

To hate or laugh cynically at religion and religious feeling in older men, poets or philosophers, is to lose sight of this truth. They are plainly men of wisdom and sensibility at least as acute as our own: they have had, too, so much more time to grow and experience. Therefore we should look carefully and interestedly at what they have to tell us of the feelings of the soul in its mid-journey and in the days when it knows the end of the road is really at hand. For as we are they were once, and we may be what they are.

*But* we do not do well to extend this consideration to all, indeed we should refuse it to most men. Only poets and philosophers may demand it from us, not fools, or the mass of mankind. And yet I think, as I write, of Bertrand Russell, who in his essay, "A Free Man's Worship," sets out from the belief, that I hold now, to construct a noble and bold religion, which is so compelling in its call and so honest in its facing of facts that it seems possible to acquiesce in it.

It is very interesting, trying to forecast one's own development. The open mind, the sensitive heart, these are what we must keep exposed to experience, for it to print on them what it may.

I never would have thought to read there what is written there now. Some month's perusal of it accustoms me to the legend, and – "I wonder what the next announcement will be."

## HIGHGATE

*Noon, Monday,* August 21st, 1916.

Dearest Lad,

I go down in an hour to the pit again, less willingly, more hating it than ever.

What I have thought and read lately and from being with you, makes me doubt very much if I do well to go. This is the bitterest part of it.

I do ill to go. I ought to fight no more. But death, I suppose, is the penalty, and public opinion and possible misunderstanding. . . You see how complicated it gets. "Thoughts were given us to conceal our passions from ourselves!" Were I to follow mine, my passions, I would not be here. But "Now is the native hue of resolution sicklied o'er with the pale cast of thought!"

I am *almost* certain I do wrong to go on – not quite certain, and anyhow, I question if I am of martyr stuff.....

Write soon,

A.G.W.

## OFFICERS AND THE WAR

### *Monday*, Sept. 11th, 1916.

I must try and make out what the officers among whom I move think of this war, its causes, its probable effects, its merits and demerits, and its remedies when it is over.

One sees, of course, that all the society in which one may at any moment find oneself is very fluid, and one doesn't like to hazard opinions, and they are not easily elicited.

I have mentioned the feeling against conscientious objectors, even in the minds of sentimental and religious people. Even R..... speaks sneeringly of Bertrand Russell; no one is willing to revise his ideas or make clear to himself his motives in joining the war; even if anybody feels regret for having enlisted, he does not like to admit it to himself Why should he? Every man, woman, and child is taught to regard him as a hero; if he has become convinced of wrong action it lands him in an awkward position which he had much better not face. So everything tends to discourage him from active thinking on this important and, in the most literal sense, vital question.

They are, as one knows, many of them worthy and unselfish men, not void of intelligence in trivial matters, and ready to carry through this unpleasant business to the end, with spirits as high as they can keep them, and as much attention to their men as the routine and disciplinary conscience of their colonel will permit.

They are not often aggressive or offensively military. This is the dismal part of it: that these men, almost the best value in the ordinary upper class that we have, should allow themselves to suppose that all this is somehow necessary and inevitable; that they should give so much labour and time to the killing of others, though to the plain appeals of poverty and inefficiency in government, as well national as international, they are so absolutely heedless. How is it that as much blood and money cannot be poured out when it is a question of saving and helping mankind rather than of slaying them?

I suppose it is the suddenness and the threat of unusually terrible destruction, when war comes, that makes men respond so willingly to this singularly uninspiring appeal when they will not listen to the Socialist.

## "WHY GO ON?"

### *Sunday*, Sept. 24th, 1916. *A Tent.*

I am very unhappy. I wish to make clear to myself why, to thrash out what my desires really tend to.

I am unhappier than I ever was last year, and this not only because I have been separated from my friends or because I am simply more tired of the war.

It is because my whole outlook towards the thing has altered. I endured what I did endure last year patiently, believing I was doing a right and reasonable thing. I had not thought out the position of the pacifist and the conscientious objector, I was always sympathetic to these people, but never considered whether my place ought not to have been rather among them than where I actually was. Then I came back to England feeling rather like the noble crusader or explorer who has given up much for his friend but who is not going to be sentimental or overbearing about it though he regards himself as somehow different from and above those who have not endured as he has done.

I have described how I modified this feeling

after much company with J..... It would certainly be much pleasanter if I could regard myself still in this rather sublime light as the man who goes into the pit for his friends: but I cannot do so, for I am beginning to think that I never ought to have gone into it at all. "This war is trivial, for all its vastness," says B. Russell, and so I feel. I am being pained, bored, and maddened – and to what end? It is the uselessness of it that annoys me. I had once regarded it as inevitable; now I don't believe it was, and had I been in full possession of my reasoning powers when the war began, I would never have joined the Army. To have taken a stand against the whole thing, against the very conception of force, even when employed against force, would have really been my happier and truer course.

The war so filled up my perspective at first that I could not see anything close because of it: most people are still like that. To find a growing body of men who can really be "au-dessus de la mêlée," who can comprehend and condemn it, who can live in the world beside the war and yet not in it, is extremely encouraging to anyone who can acclaim himself of their brotherhood. Spiritually I am of it but I am prevented from being among them. I am a creature caught in a net.

Most men fight, if not happily, at any rate patiently, sure of the necessity and usefulness of their work. So did I – once! Now it all looks to me so absurd and brutal that I can only force myself to continue in a kind of dream-state; I hypnotise myself to undergo it. What *good*, what *happiness* can be produced by some of the scenes I have had to witness in the last few days?

Even granting it was necessary to resist Germany by arms at the beginning – and this I have yet most carefully to examine – why go on?

Can no peace be concluded?

Is it not known to both armies that each is utterly weary and heartsick?

Of course it is. Then why, in God's name, go on?

It must be unreasonable to continue. The victorious, or seemingly victorious side, ought to offer peace: no peace can be worse than this bloody stupidity. The maddening thing is the sight of men of fairly goodwill accepting it all as necessary; this angers me, that men *must* go on. Why? Who wants to?

Moreover, I feel quite clearly that I ought to

have stood aside. It is these men who stand aside, these philosophers, and the so-called conscientious objectors, who are the living force of the future; they are full of the light that must come sooner or later; they are sneered at now, but their position is firm.

If all mankind were like them there would not have been war. Duty to country and King and civilisation! Nonsense! For none of these is a man to be forced to leave his humanity on one side and make a passionate destroying beast of himself. I am a man before I am anything else, and all that is human in me revolts. I would fain stand beside these men I admire, whose cause is the highest part of human nature, calm reason, and kindliness.

The argument drawn from the sufferings of the men in the trenches, from the almost universal sacrifices to duty, are not valid against this. Endurance is hard, but not meritorious simply because it is endurance. We are confronted with two sets of martyrs here: those of the trenches, and those of the tribunal and the civil prison, and not by any means are the former necessarily in the right.

And it is not even as if the Army men were

content simply to do their dirty work: they sneer at the pacifist, they encourage the sentiments of the *Spectator* and such poisonous papers, or, at any rate, they are profoundly indifferent to the cause of Internationalism; they are ready to fight and beat the Boche (as they will call him), and there is the end.

Yes! There was but one way for me, and I have seen it only when it was too late to pursue it. Even be the thing as necessary as you like, be the constitution of this world really so foul and hellish that force must be met by force, yet I should have stood aside, no brutality should have led me into it. Had I stood apart I should have stood on firm logical ground; where I was truth would have been, as it is among my friends now.

To defy the whole system, to refuse to be an instrument of it – this *I* should have done.

## COMING HOME
## TO LONDON ON LEAVE

*Wednesday*, Sept. 6th, 1916.

I have succeeded in getting leave, and write now in the back garden of M.....'s house at

Beckenham. I arrived last night about nine, very short of money, having only about 3s. to travel up from W..... to town, luckily with a ticket. We reached London about seven. The sun was setting as I crossed Waterloo bridge, a red bubble behind the Houses of Parliament, but in Waterloo station the sunlight had still been intense, though of that thick, almost palpable radiance that low sunbeams have from autumn suns seen through glass. After the journey almost the vividest happiness is over: the evernearing imminence of London, the outlying commons dotted with children's figures playing, one I remember standing up amid a bush of dark green gorse, wearing a little red Corot-like cap.

You approach the wilderness of roofs, see the tall buildings so familiar to you far away over them, the train winds and twists bumpily over points and switches, you lean out of the window and look up the long vertebrate rod of carriages, watch them turn and tail round the curves, you pass Battersea and Vauxhall, more and more widths of line, shunting engines, pointsmen, forests of signals, the signal boxes perched right up above the line; the arch of the great station opens before you dark and gloomy beneath the dirty glass, the ends of the platforms stretch forth to meet you, you wonder which it will be, this side, this side, in you glide past the long line of porters and waiting friends: you alight, everyone is welcomed, you make your way out. London! London! I think the first piece of conscious un-happiness comes when you realise how alone you are.

You have returned to London full of an immense energy and desire towards happiness. You want companionship in it. At camp when you have been happy you have been happy by being with friends mainly, by taking joy from them and by the assurance that you are returning it to them again. Here in London, you want the same kind of thing but in different terms. In camp the happiness for both is the intenser because each realises that only with and from the other can he satisfy his wants; with E..... alone, for instance, could I be happy, and I knew it was so for him. Naturally I turned to E....., and as naturally was I satisfied. Here, to whom shall I turn? Custom demands I shall turn to my family; affection demands no less that I shall turn to my friends, the friends who have always been good to me and with whom life is good. There is a well-experienced conflict in the first place. But over and above these two desires is a third, perhaps I should say that the third desire is really the only one, fulfilling itself inadequately in each of the two better identified wishes. This third desire then – I can hardly analyse it.

*Monday*, Sept. 11th, 1916.

I continue really the line of thought from what I have written above. What has come to me recently is the supreme value of human love. I have never loved my friends so much, nor rejoiced so deeply in the assurance of their love for me, as I have done during the last few weeks before coming out here. It has seemed the most blessed thing in the world to have J..... and M....., M..... and M....., A..... and H..... to love me, and to feel they know how I love them; the growing joy of this is coming to compensate me for all I lost when any vague notion of eternal and supernatural benevolence had to be abandoned. It is from man we must seek our greatest happiness, man the lover. It is plain from this that love gains a zest, is prized more highly when it is given to and taken from one whom we have chosen for ourselves, or who has chosen us. The relation of friendship becomes, in fact, more precious when it is open to one to accept or reject communion with another soul and acceptance so amply justifies itself. Going a step further from this it is evident that the pleasure of gaining affection from new sources, and pouring oneself out in new affections must be one of the greatest pleasures in life; perhaps greater than the constant renewal of old loves, though this with J..... is priceless in value.

It is this great tide of love surging up in one that prompts the feeling of loneliness when the narrow love possible in camp is widened out. This is where the third desire I spoke of enters. Love, it is felt, ought now to be given, as it were, absolutely anew. Surveying mankind one wants to choose out some recipient for true love.

# Part Four – Diary

*In September 1916 West returned to France as an officer.*

*The extracts in this part cover the time from his arrival in the trenches until his death in April 1917, a period during which he was continuously in France. The diary ends with a couple of extracts describing his happiest time in the army, while undergoing a course of training at an officers' school.*

## IN THE TRENCHES

### *Sunday*, Sept. 17th, 1916.

A tedious morning in the trenches prompts me to write down experiences and trivial little events which ordinarily I would not value enough to record, simply to pass the time. The trenches I am in are near G....., were originally German, and have been recently captured by the British. I have not been really in the trenches for a long time, and find the renewal of the experience particularly trying.

We got up here about 2.20 a.m. Sunday morning – a terribly long relief, for we started out for this line from G..... Ridge at 8.30 p.m. Saturday night. The men were dog-tired when they got here, and though ordered to dig, complied very unwillingly, and were allowed to sit about or lean on their spades, or even to stand up and fall asleep against the side of the trench. It was a smelly trench. A dead German – a big man – lay on his stomach as if he were crawling over the parades down into the trench; he had lain there some days, and that corner of trench reeked even when someone took him by the legs and pulled him away out of sight, though not

123

out of smell, into a shell-hole. We sat down and fell into a comatose state, so tired we were. On our right lay a large man covered with a waterproof, his face hidden by a sand-bag, whom we took to be a dead Prussian Guardsman, but the light of dawn showed him to be an Englishman by his uniform. From where I sit I can see his doubled-up knees

The men lay about torpidly until 4.30 a.m., when B..... ordered a stand-to. We tried to keep awake merely for form's sake while the light very slowly grew. Stand down went at 5.30, and B..... made us tea, and added rum for the others; the very smell of rum makes me sick, because it is connected with the trenches last winter.

One always feels better with daylight – of this kind of life alone is the psalmist's saying true – in ordinary modern life, where unhappiness consists so much in *mental* agitation, it is startlingly false.

We joke over the tea and biscuits, go into the next bay and talk to the men about the German things they have found and are determined to get home somehow – a rifle, a belt-buckle with "Gott mit uns" on it, a bayonet, and so on.

We try and make out where we are on the

map, and find we are at least 1,000 yards away.

Then we resolve that as we had practically no sleep last night nor the night before, and I had little even the night before that, we will try and get some. We lie . . .

### *Wednesday*, Sept. 20th, 1916.

So far I had written when it became evident that our quiet Sunday was to be of the usual kind and we were to be bombarded. H.E. shells, about 6-inch ones, came over with a tremendous black smoke, making an explosion and sending up a column of earth about thirty feet high. The first intimation I had was when I went round the corner to the next bay to see where one had fallen, and found a man with a little ferrety nose and inadequate yellow moustche, in a very long great-coat, sitting muttering away on the firing-step like a nervous rabbit and making vague gestures with his hands and head. He would return no answer to questions, and I was told two men had just been buried in a dug-out near by. I went round and found two more pale men, rather earthy. I talked to them and did my best to comfort them. A few more shells came over, unpleasandy near, but it was not yet certain whether they were definitely after us.

Soon this was clear. They worked down a winding trench, and blew in the walls; we lost six men by burying and ten others wounded or suffering from shell-shock. It was horrible. A whistle would be heard, nearer and nearer, ceasing for a mere fraction of a second when the shell was falling and about to explode. Where was it coming?

Men cowered and trembled. It exploded, and a cloud of black reek went up – in the communication trench again. You went down it; two men were buried, perhaps more you were told, certainly two. The trench was a mere undulation of newly-turned earth, under it somewhere lay two men or more. You dug furiously. No sign. Perhaps you were standing on a couple of men now, pressing the life out of them, on their faces or chests. A boot, a steel helmet – and you dig and scratch and uncover a grey, dirty face, pitifully drab and ugly, the eyes closed, the whole thing limp and mean-looking: this is the devil of it, that a man is not only killed, but made to look so vile and filthy in death, so futile and meaningless that you hate the sight of him.

Perhaps the man is alive and kicks feebly or frantically as you unbury him: anyhow, here is the first and God knows how many are not beneath him. At last you get them out, three dead, grey, muddy masses, and one more jibbering live one.

Then another shell falls and more are buried.

We tried to make them stand up.

It is noticeable that only one man was wounded; six were buried alive.

I shall always remember sitting at the head of this little narrow trench, smoking a cigarette and trying to soothe the men simply by being quiet. Five or six little funk-holes dug into the side of the trench served to take the body of a man in a very huddled and uncomfortable position, with no room to move, simply to cower into the little hole. There they sit like animals for market, like hens in cages, one facing one way, one another. One simply looks at his hands clasped on his knees, dully and lifelessly; shivering a little as a shell draws near; another taps the side of his hole with his finger-nails, rhythmically; another hides himself in his great-coat and passes into a kind of torpor. Of course, when a shell falls on to the parapet and bores down into the earth and explodes, they are covered over like so many potatoes. It is with the greatest difficulty that we can shift the men into another bit of trench and make them stand up.

I found myself cool and useful enough, though after we had been shelled for about two and a half hours on end my nerves were shaky and I could have cried for fright as each shell drew near, and longed for nothing so much as to rush down a deep cellar. I did not betray any kind of weak feeling.

It was merely consideration of the simple fact that a shell, if it did hit me, would either wound me or kill me, both of which were good inasmuch as they would put a pause to this existence – that kept me up to my standard of unconcern. And the more I experience it, the more fear seems a thing quite apart from possible consequences, which may occur in a person even when he assents fully to the proposition I have noted above.

I feel afraid at the moment. I write in a trench that was once German, and shells keep dropping near the dug-out. There is a shivery fear that one may fall into it or blow it in.

Yet *what* do I fear? I mind being killed because

I am fond of the other life, but I know I should not miss it in annihilation. It is not that I fear.

I don't definitely feel able to say I *fear* the infliction of pain or wound. I cannot bind the fear down to anything definite. I think it resolves itself simply into the realisation of the fact that being hit by a shell will produce a new set of circumstances so strange that one does not know how one will find oneself in them. It is the knowledge that something may happen with which one will not be able to cope, or that one's old resolutions of courage, &c., will fail one in this new set of experiences. Something unknown there is. How will one act when it happens? One may be called upon to bear or perform something to which one will find oneself inadequate.

The shelling went on – on this Sunday, I mean – for about five hours, and we had a few biscuits and a tot of whisky about 1 o'clock. By then the whole of the little communication trench had been battered by successive shells, and we had left off going down it after each one, as the Germans had turned machine-gun fire on to the levelled portion of trench. We stood, B....., G....., Bl....., and I, in the only undamaged bay, eating and drinking, and watching the huge columns of earth and smoke as the work of destruction went on. They had worked rather off this particular trench, and the men still stood all about it, but I believed for certain that they would return towards the end and smash in the only bay to which they would naturally have hoped to have driven us. I had had enough whisky to enable me to view this prospect with nothing but interested excitement, and really did not flinch as the shells fell, seemingly groping their way towards their mark.

Just as they drew near, a runner from the X.....'s came down to say the Germans had broken through on their left and were attacking, would we look after the third line and the flank? This news woke us all up from this rather unreal alertness of impending destruction and we rushed off with rifles, bayonets, and all manner of weapons to man the trench. No foe appeared, but it cheered us, and they did not shell very much more that night. The strain of the whole thing was very much worse than anything we had ever had at the B..... section.

## LIVING FOR THE MOMENT

### *Tuesday*, Nov. 23rd, 1916.

A grey, warmer day. The sun looked through only for a minute or two in the afternoon. We went in the evening to an estaminet on the left. After that Cl..... and I walked down the road under the moon, and talking to him then I grew more convinced of the brutalising process that was going on: how impossible it was to read, even when we had leisure, how supremely one was occupied with food and drink. Cl..... himself said he had found the same on his first campaign; it took him three weeks to get back to a state where he could read, and so it is. All my dreams of the days after the war centre round bright fires, arm-chairs, good beds, and abundant meals.

## IN AND OUT OF THE TRENCHES

### *Monday*, Sept. 25th, 1916.

A better village than we have been in yet, on the A..... River. Poplar lanes and water-meadows, and red sunsets, calm and chilling.

Moved to The C....., in a valley with a camp in it about seven miles this side of M..... A comfortable night there.

### *Tuesday*, Sept. 26th, 1916.

Moved at 8.30 towards the Front. Everybody rather fed up and tired. Reached a shell-torn ridge just near G..... about noon, and stayed there till 6 p.m. eating, drinking, and sleeping; then moved up to occupy trenches near M..... A quiet enough night, but not much sleep.

### *Wednesday*, Sept. 27th, 1916.

The French came up behind us in large numbers, very active and talkative. Daylight showed a fearful lot of dead Germans round the trench and an appalling shambles in the dug-outs.

A fairly quiet day, sunny. The French moved about all over the valley regardless of anything. We had two good meals. We were relieved at night by the French.

*Thursday*, Sept. 28th, 1916.

Left trenches at about 4.30 a.m. Fearfully tiring march back to C....., where we lived in a kind of manhole in the, trench. B....., Bl....., and I had one to ourselves, and our valises with us. Slept and fed. Read "Scholar Gipsy" and "Thyrsis" and talked about Oxford together at night. These two are the only valuable men among the officers of the Company.

*Friday*, Sept. 29th, 1916.

Rainy and depressing. Up to trenches again by T..... Wood. Seven men killed by a shell as soon as we got in the trench; beastly sight! I went up to find the way at G..... at night. I got back to find a Buszard's cake – jolly evening. Slept on the floor of a dug-out. Stomach troubles.


POINTS OF VIEW: ATHEISM

*Saturday*, Sept. 30th, 1916.

Walked through D..... Wood with B..... Wood in an unspeakable mess. The fields are all over dandelion and vetch here; the sun, of course, is in the April-May position again.

Wrote to M....., C....., and N..... We moved back a few hundred yards to B..... Wood and slept in a rough bivouac. I was very warm and comfortable. It is notable that to-night we discussed ever so slightly the problems of atheism. I had pronounced a few days ago that I was an atheist, and after a few of the usual jabs at Balliol the thing passed off. To-night I said something about my being a respectable atheist, to which it was promptly answered that there could be no such thing: and people said "You aren't really an atheist, are you?" Thus we see how men cannot get out of their minds "the horrid atheist" idea – the idea that intellectual convictions of this sort must of necessity imply some fearful moral laxity.

The most religious men are really the extreme Christians or mystics, and the atheists – nobody can understand this. These two classes have really occupied their minds with religion.

## UTTERANCES OF A GERMAN PRINCE

*Sunday*, Oct. 1st, 1916.

A fine morning; wrote to C..... We built a kind of shelter during the day, and had a pleasant day altogether; good meals, but never quite enough. Peace came near to-night in several ways and filled us with a happy contentment as we went to bed in our shelter with plenty of candles. Warmth, and a misty autumn night; fairly quiet, too, for the Front!

I received to-day a memorandum about Bertrand Russell, telling of a course of lectures he would give, and containing a statement by himself of what the W.O. had recently done to him. It showed the strength of the conscientious objector and pacifist movement, even in this welter of brute force. Then I read of an article by a German, Prince H....., on the necessity of at once stopping the war, making the usual and obvious points very well; it was good to find a German and a prince speaking so wisely.

S....., an officer here from Oxford, Nonconformist and, I think, religious, came back from a machine-gun course and remarked, half-ashamedly, that he had really come to the

135

conclusion since he had been away that the war was really very silly, and we all ought to go home.

Nobody took any notice of what he said, or else treated it laughingly; but I saw he meant it, and really had seen something new. It had come to him as a definite vision, and he was a bit disquieted. This is as it should be, and I must get talking to him.

## IN AND OUT
## OF THE TRENCHES AGAIN

### *Monday*, Oct. 2nd, 1916.

Rain. Read "Tristram Shandy" with much pleasure. *New Age* came. We sang jollily in our bivouac at night, B....., G....., and I. We slept well. S..... took a carrying party, which didn't return till 5.30 a.m. G..... came back and brought a bottle of whisky with him.

### *Tuesday*, Oct. 3rd, 1916.

Rain! Went in search of a canteen with G....., and failed to find one. Started at 3.30 in the afternoon to go up in support. Didn't arrive at our right trench till 2.30 next morning; misty and cold; very tired.

### *Wednesday*, Oct. 4th, 1916.

Rain all morning. We sat and sang. Went out at night; very fatigued! G..... came in with a working-party at 7 a.m. on Thursday morning. We were in bivouac at T..... Wood. He had great trouble with the men.

## THE COMMON VIEW

### *Thursday*, Oct. 5th, 1916.

Dull. I observed several more features in the common opinions concerning the war. G..... said: "Fancy all this trouble being brought on us by the Germans." Universal assent.

Then B....., the captain, remarked that it was really very silly to throw pieces of lead at one another, and from this someone developed the idea that our civilisation was only a surface thing, and we were savages beneath the slightest scratch.

What no one seems to see is that our country may be at any rate partially responsible, or that those who, like conscientious objectors, refuse to debase themselves to the level of savages are worthy of any respect, intellectually, if not morally.

One observes again the "It had to be!" attitude, which Hardy notes about the D'Urberville family.

So it is. People will not really move a finger to mould even their own lives outside the rules of the majority or public opinion. No one sits down to consider the rightness of his every action, and his judgments on political acton he takes from the papers.

Independent judgment in private or public affairs is the rarest thing in the world.

We did nothing all day but rest. I read "Tristram Shandy" and wrote letters. S.O.S. signals came through at night, just at dinner, and perturbed us somewhat. They were soon cancelled.

*Friday*, Oct. 6th, 1916.

Fair Arrangements made for an attack tomorrow. I was left out. I was very glad to go.

Reached the transport lines about 7 p.m. and had a good dinner and sleep.

*Saturday*, Oct. 7th, 1916.

Went off to C..... by lorry. Saw B..... walking along the road near T....., and had lunch with him and his ambulance.

C..... is a delightful town, quite small, but compact and efficient. I bought butter and cheese and fruit, and had tea at an excellent small pâtisserie. A kind of large paved hall in the fashion of the Dutch pictures gave off from behind the shop, and one fed at tables round it. There were cages of canaries there that sang lustily, and a few great dogs. These sounds, combined with laughter, quick talk, and the song of girls echoing in the spacious area, were the most pleasant thing that I had heard. I left C..... about 4.30 and got back about 7. Battalion attacked.

## AFTER THE ATTACK

### *Sunday*, Oct. 8th, 1916.

News came through on this day of heavy rain and wind of our losses in the attack. Very heavy. B....., L....., and Bl....., all killed; B....., a good blighty; G....., dangerously wounded. I never felt more utterly sick and miserable than to-day. We moved up at midnight to B..... Wood to await the Battalion's return from the trenches. They were very glorious when they came, but arrived at the sand-pits near M..... a very tired crowd, about 1.30 p.m.

### *Sunday*, Oct. 15th, 1916.

Moved from M..... It was very pleasant there in some ways: dinner was good with O....., the doctor, and parson; not bad arguments, and a good deal of freedom. I, being the only man outside headquarters who has any idea of logical abstract argument, was in the more favour.

The parson I like. He has wit and a pleasing frankness. The doctor is feline, almost Jewish and strokeable.

*Friday*, Nov. 3rd, 1916.

I sit on a high bank above a road at H..... By my side stands a quarter of a bottle of red wine at 1.50 francs the bottle. The remaining three-quarters are in my veins. I am perfectly happy physically: so much so that only my physical being asserts itself. From my toes to the very hair of my head I am a close compact unit of pleasurable sensations. Now, indeed, it is good to live; a new power, a new sensibility to physical pleasure in all my members. The whistle blows for "Fall in!" I lift the remnant of the wine to my lips and drain the dregs. All the length of the march it lasts me, and the keenness, the compactness, the intensity of perpetual well-being doesn't even leave my remotest finger-tips.

The silver veil of gossamer webs are round my hair, the juice of the autumn grape gladdening all my veins. I am the child of Nature. I wish always to be so.

## SPECIAL COURSE
## OF TRAINING IN FRANCE

### *Saturday*, Feb. 10th, 1916.

The course at F..... which I entered on at the beginning of January is now over. About twenty of us in one mess, at an inn in the rue de Th....., were my principal companions. They were of all regiments, three or four Australians, two Scotchmen, two Guardsmen, and the rest mainly North Country. Here, as usual, is the same lesson to be learnt about men in the lump. They were all very nice, and couldn't understand me. They thought I was a pro-German, a Socialist, and a Poet. Anyone who isn't at once intelligible is put down at any rate as the first of these. They are all full of petty narrow loyalties to regiment or county. I think North Country people are more intensely narrow and venomous in this way. They are all rather against America, or were when Wilson was beginning his negotiations, and talk of Yanks and yellow races. I don't think they give much thought to anything. They argue by assertions proclaimed louder than their opponents. A gramophone has occurred during the last day, and they play "The Bing Boys." But how I love them all. It is 5 o'clock and the light has just been turned on. R..... and I have spent the day since 9 a.m. waiting for 'buses up at the back gate of the White Château. 'Bus after 'bus, with lorries, too, has come up, some with officers and men for the following course, all covered with white dust, but very happy to have got here. Their kits are wheeled off in barrows by their servants into the billets where we have been sleeping for five weeks. We stand about and talk to other officers, go for slow walks out on the E..... or A..... Road: we talk of ourselves, of our natures and moods, of what we would do if we were home: we tell one another what we were doing before the war; of our friends. R..... tells me about his wife. We confide our dreams to one another; we talk of the other people in the mess and of the men in our own battalions. It is a sunny day, and against the walls and in sheltered places the heat is pleasant. Out on the E..... Road the whole of F..... lies before us; a mist is gathering over it from the surrounding hills and from the chimneys of the jute factory. Little girls pass and repass through the crowd of officers with quiet happy eyes. I am very happy. I love all the men, and simply rejoice to see them going on day by day their own jolly selves, building up such a wall of jocundity around me.

# Part Five – Poems

§ God! how I hate you, you young cheerful men! § The end of the second year § The night patrol § 'The owl abash'd' or the present estate of Oxford § Tea in the garden § The last God § Spurned by the gods § The traveller § Seeing her off § On reading ballads

# GOD! HOW I HATE YOU,
# YOU YOUNG CHEERFUL MEN!

On a University Undergraduate moved to verse by the war.

Phrases from H. Rex Feston's "Quest of Truth": Poems on Doubt, War, Sorrow, Despair, Hope, Death, Somewhere in France. He was killed in action and was an undergraduate at Exeter.

His attitude is that God is good, amused, rather, at us fighting. "Oh, happy to have lived these epic days," he writes (of us). This (he had been three years at Oxford) is his address to the Atheists:

"I know that God will never let me die.
  He is too passionate and intense for that.
See how He swings His great suns through the sky,
  See how He bammers the proud-faced mountains flat;
He takes a handful of a million years
  And flings them at the planets; or He throws
His red stars at the moon; then with hot tears
  He stoops to kiss one little earthborn rose.
Don't nail God down to rules, and think you know!
  Or God; Who sorrows all a summer's day
Because a blade of grass has died, will come
  And suck this world up in His lips, and lo!
Will spit it out a pebble, powdered grey,
  Into the whirl of Infinity's nothingless foam."

This ruined the reputation of all English Atheists for months!

GOD! How I hate you, you young cheerful men,
Whose pious poetry blossoms on your graves
As soon as you are in them, nurtured up
By the salt of your corruption, and the tears
Of mothers, local vicars, college deans,
And flanked by prefaces and photographs
From all your minor poet friends – the fools –
Who paint their sentimental elegies
Where sure, no angel treads; and, living, share
The dead's brief immortality.

                     Oh Christ!
To think that one could spread the ductile wax
Of his fluid youth to Oxford's glowing fires
And take her seal so ill! Hark how one chants –
"Oh happy to have lived these epic days" –
"These epic days"! And he'd been to France,
And seen the trenches, glimpsed the huddled dead
In the periscope, hung in the rusting wire:
Choked by their sickly fœtor, day and night
Blown down his throat: stumbled through
    ruined hearths,
Proved all that muddy brown monotony,
Where blood's the only coloured thing. Perhaps
Had seen a man killed, a sentry shot at night,
Hunched as he fell, his feet on the firing-step,
His neck against the back slope of the trench,

And the rest doubled up between, his head
Smashed like an egg-shell, and the warm grey brain
Spattered all bloody on the parados:
Had flashed a torch on his face, and known his friend,
Shot, breathing hardly, in ten minutes – gone!
Yet still God's in His heaven, all is right
In the best possible of worlds. The woe,
Even His scaled eyes must see, is partial, only
A seeming woe, we cannot understand.
God loves us, God looks down on this our strife
And smiles in pity, blows a pipe at times
And calls some warriors home. We do not die,
God would not let us, He is too "intense;"
Too "passionate," a whole day sorrows He
Because a grass-blade dies. How rare life is!
On earth, the love and fellowship of men,
Men sternly banded: banded for what end?
Banded to maim and kill their fellow men –
For even Huns are men. In heaven above
A genial umpire, a good judge of sport,
Won't let us hurt each other! Let's rejoice
God keeps us faithful, pens us still in fold.
Ah, what a faith is ours (almost, it seems,
Large as a mustard-seed) – we trust and trust,
Nothing can shake us! Ah, how good God is
To suffer us be born just now, when youth

149

That else would rust, can slake his blade in gore,
Where very God Himself does seem to walk
The bloody fields of Flanders He so loves!


## THE END OF THE SECOND YEAR

ONE writes to me to ask me if I've read
Of "the Jutland battle," of "the great advance
Made by the Russians," chiding – "History
Is being made these days, these are the things
That are worth while."

     These!

        Not to one who's lain.
In Heaven before God's throne with eyes abased,
Worshipping Him, in many forms of Good,
That sate thereon; turning this patchwork world
Wholly to glorify Him, point His plan
Toward some supreme perfection, dimly visioned
By loving faith: not these to him, when, stressed
By some soul-dizzying woe beyond his trust,
He lifts his startled face, and finds the Throne
Empty, and turns away, too drunk with Truth
To mind his shame, or feel the loss of God.

150

## THE NIGHT PATROL

France, March 1916.

OVER the top! The wire's thin here, unbarbed
Plain rusty coils, not staked, and low enough:
Full of old tins, though – "When you're
   through, all three,
Aim quarter left for fifty yards or so,
Then straight for that new piece of German wire;
See if it's thick, and listen for a while
For sounds of working; don't run any risks.
About an hour; now, over!"
                   And we placed
Our hands on the topmost sand-bags, leapt, and stood
A second with curved backs, then crept to the wire,
Wormed ourselves tinkling through, glanced
   back, and dropped
The sodden ground was splashed with shallow pools,
And tufts of crackling cornstalks, two years old,
No man had reaped, and patches of spring grass.
Half-seen, as rose and sank the flares, were strewn
With the wrecks of our attack: the bandoliers,
Packs, rifles, bayonets, belts, and haversacks,
Shell fragments, and the huge whole forms of shells
Shot fruitlessly – and everywhere the dead.
Only the dead were always present – present

151

As a vile sickly smell of rottenness;
The rustling stubble and the early grass,
The slimy pools – the dead men stank through all,
Pungent and sharp; as bodies loomed before,
And as we passed, they stank: then dulled away
To that vague fœtor, all encompassing,
Infecting earth and air. They lay, all clothed,
Each in some new and piteous attitude
That we well marked to guide us back: as he,
Outside our wire, that lay on his back and crossed
His legs Crusader-wise; I smiled at that,
And thought on Elia and his Temple Church.
From him, at quarter left, lay a small corpse,
Down in a hollow, huddled as in bed,
That one of us put his hand on unawares.
Next was a bunch of half a dozen men
All blown to bits, an archipelago
Of corrupt fragments, vexing to us three,
Who had no light to see by, save the flares.
On such a trail, so lit, for ninety yards
We crawled on belly and elbows, till we saw,
Instead of lumpish dead before our eyes,
The stakes and crosslines of the German wire.
We lay in shelter of the last dead man,
Ourselves as dead, and heard their shovels ring
Turning the earth; then talk and cough at times.

152

A sentry fired and a machine-gun spat;
They shot a flare above us, when it fell
And spluttered out in the pools of No Man's Land,
We turned and crawled past the remembered dead:
Past him and him, and them and him, until,
For he lay some way apart, we caught the scent
Of the Crusader and slid past his legs,
And through the wire and home, and got our rum.

## 'THE OWL ABASH'D'

### OR

## THE PRESENT ESTATE OF OXFORD
### (considered in the Augustan Manner)

MEANWHILE the Toga (Tully's phrase forgot)
Makes way for arms; the muses hover not
As they were wont o'er Oxford's day and night
With calm usurpance and self-conscious right:
Athene's Owl once held prescriptive roost
In every hall and College, and was used
With academic hoot to calm abode
From Eastern Iffley up to Southmoor Road:
The great War-eagle, subject of her ban,
Was weaken'd to a mild ey'd Pelican,
Peck'd his own breast, and dropp'd a joyful tear

When heroes compass'd fifteen Drills a year!
  But now the sapient Fowl, with staring eyes
And loud 'tu-whoo,' upbraids th' unlistening skies:
To Pallas' shoulder flies she, there to stand –
Mail'd is the shoulder, gauntleted the hand.
She drops abash'd, and wings along The High,
Calling her brood with supplicating cry: –
"Come, come, my Owlets, as in former days,
Ye Undergraduates and proud B.A.'s;
Hear Carfax chime, nine hours of day are sped!
Why come ye not? – Of course, they're all abed!"
Reliev'd she sigh'd, and seem'd to hear their snores,
To hear scouts hammering at a thousand doors,
To know those waking dreams of shadow'd pools,
Punts, girls, Eights, waistcoats, Proctors,
    dogs and Schools;
She seems to see the breakfast-table laid,
To scent the coffee and the marmalade,
His social song the genial kettle trolls,
The eggs and bacon warm before the coals,
A morning paper, decently inane,
Lies by the plate, to soothe the waken'd brain
Blest by such unobtrusive servile art
The days of comfort comfortably start.
  "And yet I dreamt," the shuddering creature said,
"My bowers were rifled and my children fled;

154

The Heavens disdain'd me; Pallas' self was cold,
Yet, when Mars ogled her, she did not scold;
With din of arms rang all th' ethereal clime,
And tramp of deities a-marking time!
Yes, 'twas a nightmare; ah, peace-loving men,
That rise at nine and walk The High at ten,
To flaunt your socks or buy a straight-grain'd briar,
Then back to doze, with Livy, by the fire,
Here none need quake, where Sleep embraces all
At shadow-armies, marching on the wall;
To fretted minds, untun'd by Lift's debate,
Ye are, indeed, a draught mandragorate!"
   Thus far the Owl; then gently bends her flight
Where streaks of Keble vivify the sight;
Keble that rose, as Venus from the main,
In foamy spumings of a monstrous brain.
She reach'd the Parks; but what a sight was there!
Her swooning weight scarce can her pinions bear.
These peaceful Parks, where chattering nursemaids talk,
Where mail-carts flock, like Kensington's Broad Walk,
Where, until now, Dons' babies stumbling ran,
And consecrated all to Peter Pan –
Bristle with horrid arms, converted thus
From field of Peace to Campus Martius.
She scann'd this host of lithe, brown-feather'd fowl
For something with a likeness to an owl;

But there was none; she knew them eaglets all
Of her unmindful, heedless of her call.
In charge of sections or platoons they rant
Those previous souls before immersed in Kant;
Those who taught Pompey how to play his cards
Hope soon to fight their 'Cæsar' in the Guards.
Forlorn she sees the warlike feathers' tips
In act of sprouting on the upper lips.
"Undone," she shriek'd, "my nightmare all
   too true!"
Then off she flapp'd, with dismal
   "tu-whoo-whoo."

December 1914.


## TEA IN THE GARDEN

You see this Tea, no milk or sugar in it,
Like peat-born water's brown translucency,
Where deep and still it lingers through the shade
Of hazel curtains: Well, this liquid jewel,
This quiet, self-contained, smooth, rounded pool,
This glowing agaric, gold-threaded dusk,
Tranquilly dreaming, yet shot every way,
By rays of china-filtered sunlight, steam

Gliding in banks, whirling in eddied dances
Over the polished floor, now leaping off it
In restless clouds that win a kiss of the sun
Ere a death, like Semele's, from the levin-brand,
Whisk them to dissolution; this brimmed cup,
Let us pretend that it's a human mind
That we've created, for we poured it out,
Aye! and will spill it if we like – this mind,
A young man's mind, clean, unadulterate,
And noble, too, as China-tea minds are –
None of your vulgar one-and-fourpennies –
We'll govern as the gods do govern us.
He's happy now, the man: wits clean, blood warm,
And dim delightful clouds of sunlit visions,
Like steam, are born and die in loveliness
Continuously.
        But he's not fit to drink,
Needs milk and sugar, and we poured him out
The best of Tea in a biscuit-china cup,
Because we meant to drink him; milk and sugar
Will rather stultify his Attic salts
And cloud the clearness of his intellect –
But we are gods, he's ours and not his own,
So pass the milk-jug and the sugar-bowl!
Ah! how he lies and sweetly meditates,
Fond fool, those fair reflections in his mind;

Slow clouds and passing wings and leaves a-flicker,
Like little yellow flames, on the poplar tree,
And weaves an intricate theology
From the silver tea-pot spout, that gave him birth,
Your hand and wrist, jewelled and braceleted,
Behind the pot, well-wishing deities
That made him out of love, will care for him,
And bring him home at last.

                        Pour in some milk!
His light is dimmed, for quite impermeable
Is this dull muddy fluid to the sun:
Where are his glinting sparkles, amber glows,
The glazed clearness of his mirror-like soul,
As sharp reflecting as Narcissus' well?
His blood runs colder, no more leaping clouds
Of vaporous spring to gaze on the sun,
And perish gazing; he's turned "practical"
(His own word that), must keep his energies
For the lukewarm days, when lift is on the lees.
Pour in more milk: the cold white heaviness
Drops clean through all his being, re-ascends
Like monstrous births from wind impregnate
    wombs
In cloudy humours: like a witch's cauldron
His brain boils up in vaporous melancholy,
And pallid phantoms hold in it high revel

Of tireless whirling orgy.
$\qquad\qquad\qquad$ Sugar him!
And a few bubbles of air, like noisome gas,
Come popping up, and dully burst; a sweet
Faint opiate apathy distils about
His goblin-haunted soul. Thick fatty blobs
Of yellow cream o'erlay his seething brain
And spread a general obscuration;
Drawing a veil betwixt him and the world
Of mirrorable beauty – a wrinkled rind,
Like skin on a hag's cheek, that shows you still,
Crinkling and creasing in fantastic flickers,
The weary ebb and flow of his sick mind.
Come, let us end it!
$\qquad\qquad\qquad$ Take that silver spoon,
And stab him to the soul; the agony
Of its entrance may confound his fond beliefs
Concerning us, who made him, and a flame
Of purifying hatred cauterise
His poisoned being, such a flame as we
Might wince at if, between our separate worlds
Were any commerce found.
$\qquad\qquad\qquad\qquad$ Well struck! he's dead;
And only posthumous nervous energy
Still sends the cream, and bubbles floating round.
Here is no form, nor vestige of a mind.

Drink him! You take no sugar? No, nor I,
Of course! Well, pour him on the grass, we two
Are not gods yet, to torture what we rule,
And then find joy in the mangled body. Tea!
Pour out more Tea, and let's pretend no more.


## THE LAST GOD

ALL Gods are dead, even the great God Pan
Is dead at length; the lone inhabitant
Of my ever-dwindling Pantheon. Pan! Pan!
With what persistency I worshipped thee!
I saw a little crumpled clover leaf
Starring the trench side greenly, or I heard
A morning lark, and thou wast at my side
Smoothing thy child's hair; 'gainst thy curled flank
Pillowing my loving head; when God and Christ
Abandoned me, thy universal temple
Was still my home, and I of all thy flock
Was welcome there; I think that I adored thee
As few have ever done.

                           My soul this spring
Thrilled with a fuller music to thy touch,
That seemed to me more loving than of old,
When most I needed love. O love, love, love!

160

Love in the ruins, love in toil and war,
Love in decay of lovers, love in death!
1 deemed Love walked with me, Love crowned
    with life
Of flower and bird and laughter of clear streams,
And the new springing wheat.
                    Now art thou changed
To a foul witch; thou art no Circe now,
But Lachesis or Atropos, that whippeth
The tortured trees to anguish, killeth joy
Of bird and leaf and flower. Thy cynic glance
Sours my old love to hatred; thy caresses
Cause me to shudder; all thy colour, song,
Are crude and heartless. Woo me! Woo me now
As I wooed thee once; but I think that I,
I shall walk on, head high, nor hear thee more.


## SPURNED BY THE GODS


LAST night, O God, I climbed up to thy house
So loving-passionate towards thee, that not
The sharp loose flintstones hurt my feet, the blood
That the sword-grasses and low brambles drew
Whipping my ankles, flowed without a smart.
The moment lent me wings, and poured divine

And glowing ichor pelting through my veins
Chasing the slow cold blood; hot blinding torrents
Of irised glory beat upon my eyes,
And in my throbbing ears there did arise
The mighty shouts of Gods at festival.
There I, thy daughter, thy frail child, half-dead
From my great love of thee, choking with sobs
And panting lungs, my soul rapt to the sphere
Where quires the eternal music, my poor body
Affrighted that these ears should drink the hymns
Of Gods and Heroes, lowly on my knees
I crouched before thee, and resigned my life
To thee, o'erpowered by the trembling ecstasy
Of deity's completest immanence.
I waited: hardly breathing, hour on hour
Through the peering night, wishing that all
   the strength
Of thine unshamèd myriad-formed desire
And manly fervour, might delight in me,
And like the sacred fire, seize me and so
Consume me utterly.
                  Oh, sweet renown
Of Danæ and Europa! Fierce white bull,
Would I have asked thee mercy? Mercy! I,
I would have bared my breast to horns and hoofs
And joyed to feel thy hot breath on my face,

162

To have thee gore and trample me, to die
A kneaded quivering mass, thy splendid horns
And swinging dewlap dripping hot with blood.
Or hadst thou come as erst to Danæ – gold
In heavy stunning cataracts, red gold
Beating me down, staining the lilied skin,
As summer hailstorms ravish the frail vines,
Stamping them in churned mud: would I have
   whimpered
'Neath the tremendous lashes of thy love?
Nay, as I fainted into happy death,
Smothered in the embraces of thy golden arms,
A panting reef of gold, each several piece
Would seem to lie upon me like a rose,
And I should dream I was a child again
Buried in cowslips.
             This was what I prayed.
I offered thee no empty sacrifices,
No locks of hair, nor entrails of a brute,
I offered thee myself, my loveliness,
I kept it all or thee, I was not timid,
Not coy before the King of Gods – and thou,
Thou drab uxorious tyrant, sate at feast,
Champing the meat, and craned thy neck,
   and leered
Upon me, naked on the ground, then beckoned

To Juno and in suasive wheedling tones
Murmuring in her ear, pointed to me,
Thy silly sentimental votary;
And all the gods flocked round, as once they did
Round Aphrodite, strained in golden mesh
To Ares' flanks: "Loud laughter shook the sides
Of all the blessed gods" – The blessed gods! And I
Grew cold and fearful, my dishevelled hair
Was damp with dew, the fires of adoration
Flickered, burnt blue, and died in smoky doubt.
Thou had'st not come: once more thou had'st not
     come;
Once more I stumbled through the cold dead light
Of windy dawn, along the rocky path;
No little stone but stabbed now, no sly blade
Of grass or bramble but deliberately
Sawed through my skin until I cried.

                                    I lurked
Deep in the wild wood, durst not face the eyes
Of the village folk – but thee I could not fly.
Thou took'st a satyr's form, from every shadow
Glinted thy grinning teeth, I heard thy laugh
In the cry of the magpie, mocking thy poor dupe.
The burden of intolerable shame
That thou hast bound on me, thou wilt not touch
To lighten with thy finger –

## THE TRAVELLER

Oh, I came singing down the road
  Whereon was nought perplext me,
And Pan with Art before me strode,
  And Walter Pater next me.

I garnered my "impresssons" up,
  Lived in each lovely feature,
"I burned with a hard gemlike flame"
  And sensitized my nature.

We wandered up and down La Beauce
  Along the castled river,
Where rarely came the deathly frost
  To fright us to a shiver.

Till at a corner of the way
  We met with maid Bellona,
Who joined us so imperiously
  That we durst not disown her.

My three companions coughed and blushed,
  And as the time waxed later,
One murmured, pulling out his watch,
  That he must go – 'twas Pater.

And very soon Art turned away
  Huffed at Bellona's strictures,
Who hurried us past dome and spire
  And wouldn't stay for pictures.

But old Pan with his satyr legs
  Trotted beside us gamely,
Till quickening pace and rougher road
  Made him go somewhat lamely.

The rents in the La Bassée road,
  The cracks between the cobbling,
The wet communication trench,
  They set poor Pan a-hobbling.

He couldn't stand the shells and mud,
  The sap-head or the crater,
He used to say the very rats
  "Went some 'ow agin Nater."

When we were back behind Bethune
  In comfortable billets,
We two would greet the advancing Spring
  As she sailed up the rillets.

And lie 'neath the fantastic trees
   To hear the thrushes quiring,
Till young Bellona smelt us out
   And startled Pan with firing.

My heart bled for the kindly god
   Who'd sought so long to serve me,
And so I sent him back again:
   He prayed "Might heaven preserve me."

I went unto the martial maid,
   Who laughed to see me lonely,
"We're rid of them at last" she said,
   "Now I'll be honoured only."

And still we fare her road alone
   In foul or sunny weather:
Dare is that road of man or god
   Which we run on to-gether.

## SEEING HER OFF

A WHISTLE 'mid the distant hills
   Shattered the silence grey,
She turned on me her great sad eyes,
Then lightly skimmed away.

I followed slow her flying feet
   In idlest heaviness,
But, oh! my heart it laughed to see
   Roar through the proud express.

In the after silence and the gloom
   I found her there again,
And won three minutes more delight
   Before the second pain.

## ON READING BALLADS

In June 1915, having week-end leave from W..... Camp, in Surrey, I spent the Sunday with my sister roaming through the moors and woods round Rickmansworth and the Chalfonts. We had not seen one another for many months, and in close conversation forgot all the world except our two selves. This experience of intimate aloofness reached its climax when, having missed the train at a wayside station – a chance which meant my being late in my return to Camp – we lay down in a field by the track and, waiting for the train, read ballads to one another. The sudden rediscovery of the verse quoted – a sixteenth-century anonymous lyric – so intense, personal, and modern in its vivid cry, among the long objective ballads, startled us both back to the world of pains and desires, where we two must leave one another, and she return to School and I to Camp and the Army.

We lay upon a flowery hill
  Close by the railway lines,
Apollo dusting gold on us
Between the windy pines.

We watched the London trains go by
  Full of the weary folk,
Who travelled back that Sunday night
  To six more days of smoke.

They stared out at the whirling fields,
    And when they saw us two,
They turned their heads to follow us
    Till we were snatched from view,

The year was at the summer's spring
    When grass is fresh and long,
And flowers are more in bud than bloom,
    And cuckoos slacken song.

The sainfoin and the purple vetch
    Nodding above our lair
Sighed on the western breeze, whose might
    Could barely stir our hair.

The hawkweed on our ballad book
    Sprinkled its pollen fine,
And now and then a beetle dropped
    And wandered through a line.

"Sir Patrick Spens" we loitered down,
    "Tam Lin" and "Young Beichan;'
And almost felt the sunshine weep
    For the "Lass of Lochroyan."

Stanza on stanza endlessly
From her lips or from mine
Benumbed our dreaming souls, like drops
    Of a Circean wine.

I watched her while she read to me,
    As children watch their nurse,
Until my being throbbed to hear
    This solitary verse:

"O western wind, when wilt thou blow
    That the small rain down can rain?
Christ! That my love were in my arms
    And I in my bed again!"

*       *       *

The little verse cut through the twists
    Of the dream-twinèd spell,
And "Robin Hood" sank back again
    With the "Wife of Usher's Well."

And an illimitable desire
    Quickened our souls with pain.
We knew that we were still at one
    With the people in the train.